Study skills for 11–14 year-olds

Studywise 1

John Foster

📖 Collins Educational

An Imprint of HarperCollins*Publishers*

Published in 1996 by Collins Educational
An imprint of HarperCollins*Publishers*
77-85 Fulham Palace Road
Hammersmith
London W6 8JB

ISBN 0 00 320188 0

Reprinted 1996, 1997, 1998, 1999

Designed by Glynis Edwards
Cover illustration by Mike Moran
Internal illustration by Adrian Barclay (Behive Illustration) pp5, 9, 10, 11, 36, 43, 50 & 58, Kathy Baxendale pp15, 22, 23, 26, 31, 38, 39, 40, 49 & 55, Mike Moran pp45, 52 & 53, Clyde Pearson p8, Francis Scappaticci (Maggie Mundy Illustration Agency) pp6, 42, 47, 48 & 59, Harry Venning pp12, 18, 51, 54, 56 & 57.
Handwriting by Alice Bradbury, Katy Bradbury, Amy Druce, Lexi Reeve, Ben Savours, Julie Sukkar.

Printed in Hong Kong

Commissioning Editor Domenica de Rosa
Editor Louisa Coulthurst

ACKNOWLEDGEMENTS

The following publishers, authors and agents are thanked for permission to reproduce extracts and copyright material:

Children's Britannica for the extracts on *Barbados* p21, *United Nations* pp24 & 25 and *Smelting Iron* p27.

Emma Holden for her helpsheet on writing speeches p46.

Elaine Williams and *The Independent* for the extract on Kelly's vocational course p61.

HarperCollins for the screens from *The Times Electronic World Map and Database*.

OUP for the Library flow chart p15 and the extract on Jamaica p21 from *The Oxford Children's Encyclopedia*.

SEAC for the Science test paper, tier 5-7 for Key Stage 3 p50.

Stanley Thornes for the extract from *New Steps in Religious Education Book 1* by Michael Keene p19.

Sue Walker for adapted text from her leaflet *Desktop Publishing for Teachers* p40, which is available from Reading and Language Information Centre, University of Reading.

The following are thanked for permission to reproduce photographs:

Jennie Woodcock, Reflections Photo Library p4
David Rose p19
British Steel p27
Manning, Selvage & Lee Ltd p20
Paul Rose Photography and Sonal Mapara p39
Torino Mauritius, Ace Photo Agency p37
Colin Burt, Ace Photo Agency p40

Every effort has been made to contact owners of copyright material but if any have been inadvertently overlooked the publishers wil be pleased to make the necessary arrangements at the first opportunity.

CONTENTS

Introduction

How this book can be used

Studywise 1 is planned so that it can be used in a variety of ways. It can be used in schools either as a separate course on study skills within a school's tutorial programme or integrated within a school's personal and social education programme.

Alternatively, you can use it on your own or work through it with a friend or member of your family. Since each of the units deals with a separate topic, they can be worked through in any particular order, according to your own personal needs.

What this book is about

Studywise 1 is designed to help you to develop the skills you need in order to succeed in the subjects you are studying between the ages of 11 and 14. The book is divided into eleven units offering practical advice on how to develop the skills that will enable you to perform to the best of your ability in your lessons and in any tests or examinations that you may have to take.

The information and the activities in the units are designed to help you:

- to think about how you learn;
- to take responsibility for your own learning;
- to develop the skills that will enable you to study effectively;
- to identify your strengths so that you can decide which subjects you want to study in the future.

Study skills and the National Curriculum

Between the ages of 11 and 14, you will be studying the National Curriculum. This means that you will have lessons in the three core subjects – English, Maths and Science – and the seven foundation subjects – Technology (Design & Technology and Information Technology), a Modern Foreign Language, History, Geography, Art, Music and P.E. You will also have R.E. lessons and, in many schools, you may have a regular Personal and Social Education lesson.

In each of these subjects, you will be learning particular skills. For example, in Science you will be learning the skills of how to observe and

investigate. In Geography, you will be learning how to draw and interpret maps.

Study skills differ from subject skills, because they do not apply to one specific subject. They are techniques that you can use to help you to learn in *any* subject. Study skills involve planning and organising your time, developing your reading strategies, learning how to take notes and how to revise for tests.

It is important to develop your study skills for a number of reasons. First, improving your study skills will help you to improve your grades. Secondly, it will save you time and effort by making your studying more efficient.

What study skills do I need to learn?

1 How to manage your time

The key to successful studying is planning and organisation.

When they start getting homework, lots of young people find it hard to find the time to get it done. **Unit 1** will help you to understand the need for homework, and help you to organise your time to be able to get it done.

2 How to find information

If you are asked to research a topic and you do not know how to go about finding the information you need, it is easy to get frustrated. Knowing how to find information in a library, how to access information from computers, and how to collect information from people are very important study skills. **Units 2** and **6** will help you to develop these skills.

3 How to learn from books and other sources of information

Once you have found the information you want, you need to have the skills to be able to learn from it by extracting and recording the relevant facts and ideas. **Units 3** and **4** will help you to do this.

4 How to communicate facts, ideas and opinions

You need to be able to show that you have understood what you have learned by speaking and writing about it. Being able to communicate information and to express your ideas and opinions are two very important study skills. **Unit 7** will help you with oral work, and **Unit 5** with written work, including spelling and punctuation. **Unit 6** teaches you how to present your work well using a word processor. In **Unit 8** there is a section on how to answer questions in tests.

5 How to revise and recall what you have learned

If you do not make notes on what you have read, seen or heard, it can be very difficult to remember it later. **Unit 4** teaches you how to make good notes. There are also a number of techniques you can use to help you to remember the facts you need to learn for tests and examinations. **Unit 8** will help you with revising and memorising.

6 How to review your progress

Thinking about what you have learned and about the skills you have developed is useful for two reasons: it helps you to realise what you have achieved and enables you to think about what you still need to learn. **Unit 9** will help you to review your progress, identify your strengths and weaknesses, and to set yourself goals and targets for the future.

7 How to make decisions about what to study in the future

As you go through school, you will be faced with certain choices about which subjects and courses you want to study. At 14, you will have to choose which subjects you want to study for GCSE, and may also have to decide whether or not you want to take a GNVQ course. **Unit 10** is designed to get you to think about what your skills and interests are, which careers you are currently interested in and what opportunities there are for you at 16+. While **Unit 11** offers advice on how to make decisions, and looks at choosing your options, explaining what the consequences of particular choices can be.

1 Getting the homework habit

PLANNING AND ORGANISING YOUR HOMEWORK

Homework! Who cares?

Sally and Jenny are friends, but they are in different forms. Each afternoon after school they meet at the gate to walk home together.

You're late! Where've you been?

I stayed behind to see Mrs. Shepherd.

What've you been up to? Did you smash a test-tube?

No. I wanted to ask about the homework. I wasn't sure what to do.

Homework. You don't want to worry about that. That's no problem.

What do you mean?

If you don't understand it, find someone who does and copy theirs.

But...

Hey, look, there's our Janice. I'm going round her house, before going to the club. Do you want to come?

Not tonight, Jenny. I've too much to do.

You're becoming a real pain, you are. You've got this whole homework business out of proportion!

No, I haven't. You know what they said. If we want to get our GCSE's, we need to start working for them now!

GCSE's! They're five years away! Well, if you're not coming, I guess I'll just have to find someone who will. See you around.

As Jenny walks away, Sally wonders what to do. What if Jenny rings up Tina, and Tina agrees to go? Where will that leave Sally...?

IN PAIRS

What do you think Sally should do? Should she stay in and do her homework and risk losing Jenny's friendship? Or should she leave the homework and go out with Jenny?

What do you think of **a)** Jenny's attitude to homework **b)** Sally's attitude to homework?

WHY IS HOMEWORK IMPORTANT?

'Homework is important because it teaches you skills that you are going to need throughout your life. It teaches you how to study on your own and how to learn things for yourself.'   *Headteacher*

'It makes sure children learn the things they need in order to do well at school and to pass exams.'   *Parent*

'Homework is important because children can practise the skills they've learned in the lesson and finish off work that they've begun in class.'   *Teacher*

'Homework helps you to learn, because you have to think things through and put them into your own words.'   *Pupil*

'It enables us to keep a track of what our children are doing at school and what progress they are making.'   *Parent*

'Homework is a useful means of checking up that everyone has understood and learned what you've been teaching in the lesson.'   *Teacher*

'If you didn't get homework you wouldn't bother about paying attention in class.'   *Pupil*

●●● IN GROUPS ●●●

● Discuss whether homework is important.

● Study the views of pupils, parents and teachers (left) and think of other reasons why homework is important.

●●●● IN CLASS ●●●●

Choose someone in your group to note down your ideas and then share them in a class discussion.

▢ FOR YOUR FOLDER ▢

Write a statement giving your views on homework and why you think it is important, and put it in your folder.

KEEPING A HOMEWORK DIARY

Study these extracts from Katharine's and Jodie's homework diaries.

Katharine's diary

Tuesday 4 October
English – Draft a letter to a newspaper giving your views on an issue that concerns you e.g. animal rights. Due in friday.
French – Finish exercise on page 47. Learn vocabulary on page 48 for test next week.

Jodie's diary

Tuesday – Write a letter
          – Finish off French

●● IN PAIRS ●●

● Talk about the differences between Katharine's and Jodie's diary entries.

● Discuss the importance of making sure that you always write down the details of each homework and make a note of when it is due.

● Look at the entries in your own homework diaries. Are they more like Katharine's or Jodie's?

●◗● ROLE PLAY ●◗●

Role play a scene in which two friends argue about the value of homework diaries. One thinks they are a waste of time, the other tries to convince her that they are a useful way of knowing what homework you've got and when it's due.

HOMEWORK – SOME QUESTIONS AND ANSWERS

BEST PLACE?

Q: WHERE'S THE BEST PLACE TO DO YOUR HOMEWORK?

A: It depends on how much space you've got at home and whether or not you have to share a bedroom. If you can, it's worth making a corner of your bedroom into a work space, with a desk or worktop and some shelves where you can keep all your books and equipment. However, if there isn't enough space you may have to do your homework on a table in the kitchen or in the living room.

The most important thing is to try to find somewhere that's quiet, where you can concentrate and where you won't be interrupted. Also, it's important to have a flat surface on which to put your exercise books so that you can write properly. Don't try to do a written homework while you're sitting on the sofa with the book in your lap.

If you find it difficult to do your homework at home, then try working at your local library or your school library where you will be able to find the information you need if you get stuck.

BEST TIME?

Q: WHAT'S THE BEST TIME TO DO YOUR HOMEWORK?

A: That's really up to you. Often, it's impossible to do homework at a set time each day because of other commitments. The important thing is to plan your evenings and weekends so that you leave enough time to get your homework done. One way of planning your time is to make a weekly study schedule (like the one below) showing what your after-school activities are for each day and when you plan to do your homework.

One thing you shouldn't do is leave it to the last minute. It's no good trying to do your homework on the way to school on the bus in the morning or in a few minutes at registration time.

	Morning	Afternoon	Evening
Saturday	skateboarding	shopping	disco
Sunday	relaxing	maths/science	read English book

	3:30 - 4:30	4:30 - 5:30	5:30 - 6:30	6:30 - 7:30	7:30 - 8:30	8:30 - 9:30
MONDAY	come home	play tennis	eat dinner	do history	do French	watch TV
TUESDAY	come home; do geography	practice piano	eat dinner	visit best friend	write essay	have bath
WEDNESDAY	come home; watch TV	study spelling	go swimming	eat dinner	do maths	read book

Q: SHOULD YOU GET OTHER PEOPLE TO HELP YOU WITH YOUR HOMEWORK?

A: There's no harm in discussing your homework with other people, such as your friends or relatives, if it helps you to sort out your ideas. Similarly, it's worth asking for help if you get stuck. But there's no point in getting someone else to do your homework for you or copying their homework, because you won't learn anything if you do.

If you do get an awful lot of help with a piece of homework, then it's best to tell your teacher. Otherwise your teacher might not realise you are finding something difficult and therefore not give you the help you need to understand it.

Q: HOW MUCH TIME SHOULD YOU SPEND ON YOUR HOMEWORK?

A: There's no point in dashing off your homework as quickly as possible. If you do, you won't make the improvements you should or get the grades you are capable of getting. Most schools issue homework timetables which tell you how much time you are meant to spend on a particular subject each night. If you find that you are spending much longer on some subjects, then it's worth letting your teachers know. For example, you can indicate how much of the homework you've done in the time you are expected to spend on it by putting a note in the margin. People work at different speeds, and your teachers may be able to suggest ways of tackling the work that will help you to speed up.

Q: WHAT SHOULD YOU DO IF INTERRUPTIONS DISTURB YOUR HOMEWORK?

A: Sometimes, you can't help getting interrupted while you are doing your homework. What's important is how you deal with the interruption. For example, if it is someone on the telephone then you can always say that you will ring them back. Try to establish with your family and friends that once you've settled down to work, then you don't want to be interrupted unless it really is urgent.

OTHER PEOPLE?

HOW MUCH TIME?

INTERRUPTIONS?

●●● IN GROUPS ●●●

● Talk about when and where you do your homework.

● How long do you spend on your homework?

● Do other people help you with your homework?

● Discuss the advice on this page.

● Which pieces of advice do you find the most helpful?

●●●● IN CLASS ●●●●

Choose someone to act as spokesperson for your group and share your ideas in a class discussion.

●●○ ROLE PLAY ○●●

Role play a scene in which two friends argue about the value of study schedules.

☐ FOR YOUR FOLDER ☐

Look at the example study schedule, make your own and fill it in for next week, putting in all your after-school activities and the times when you plan to do your homework.

YOU AND YOUR HOMEWORK

A TEST-YOURSELF QUIZ

Do this quiz to find out about your homework habits. Keep a record of your answers and use the score-chart to work out your score.

1 When a homework is set do you write down the details in your homework diary?

a Usually ☐   b Sometimes ☐   c Never ☐

2 Do you check your bag at the end of each day to make sure you have all the books etc. you need for that evening's homework?

a Usually ☐   b Sometimes ☐   c Never ☐

3 Do you work out a plan each evening of how you are going to spend your time and when you are going to do your homework?

a Usually ☐   b Sometimes ☐   c Never ☐

4 Before starting your homework, do you check your homework diary to see what the homework is and when it's due in?

a Usually ☐   b Sometimes ☐   c Never ☐

5 Do you find it hard to get started, because you can't find all the things you need?

a Usually ☐   b Sometimes ☐   c Never ☐

6 Do you do your homework while watching TV?

a Usually ☐   b Sometimes ☐   c Never ☐

7 Do you let yourself be interrupted once you've started doing your homework?

a Usually ☐   b Sometimes ☐   c Never ☐

8 Do you put off doing your homework until the last minute?

a Usually ☐   b Sometimes ☐   c Never ☐

9 If you get stuck, do you give up rather than try to find someone to ask for help?

a Usually ☐   b Sometimes ☐   c Never ☐

10 Do you read your work through before you hand it in to be marked?

a Usually ☐   b Sometimes ☐   c Never ☐

11 If you are learning something for a test, do you ask someone to help you by testing you?

a Usually ☐   b Sometimes ☐   c Never ☐

12 Do you hand your homework in on time?

a Usually ☐   b Sometimes ☐   c Never ☐

HOW TO SCORE

Add up the points for your answers from the chart below.

Question 1	**a**	2	**b**	1	**c**	0
Question 2	**a**	2	**b**	1	**c**	0
Question 3	**a**	2	**b**	1	**c**	0
Question 4	**a**	2	**b**	1	**c**	0
Question 5	**a**	0	**b**	1	**c**	2
Question 6	**a**	0	**b**	1	**c**	2
Question 7	**a**	0	**b**	1	**c**	2
Question 8	**a**	0	**b**	1	**c**	2
Question 9	**a**	0	**b**	1	**c**	2
Question 10	**a**	2	**b**	1	**c**	0
Question 11	**a**	2	**b**	1	**c**	0
Question 12	**a**	2	**b**	1	**c**	0

WHAT YOUR SCORE MEANS

19-24

You are developing good homework habits. You are organised, you keep a check of what your homework is, and you don't waste time because you haven't got the right books and equipment. You should be able to complete your homework and have plenty of time to do the other things you like doing. If that's not the case, then think carefully about whether your homework is taking up so much time that it's getting you down, then talk to either your parents or your tutor about it.

13-18

Sometimes you are doing the right things, but you're not doing them regularly enough. You need to try to become a bit more organised in order to make sure you know what's required and to make the best use of your time. If you do, you'll find not only that you get your homework done more easily, but that your grades improve and that you have more time to do all those other things that you enjoy doing.

Go through your answers, look at the times you answered 'Sometimes' and think about what you need to do in order to be able to change the answers into 'Usually'.

0-12

You either don't think homework's all that important or you haven't yet learned how to organise yourself in order to get your homework done. If you are going to improve your homework habits then you need to make a determined effort to do something about it. You need to change your attitude and approach, but nothing will happen unless you want it to do so. Talk to your tutor and your parents and decide what you need in order to improve your homework habits.

••••••••••••••••••••••••••••••••

IN PAIRS

Talk about what you have learned from this activity about your homework habits.

FOR YOUR FOLDER

Draw up lists of good homework habits and bad homework habits.

ORGANISING AND PRESENTING YOUR HOMEWORK

How you organise and present your homework is very important. On the page opposite are examples of two homeworks. Both Ben and Vanessa were asked to make notes on the causes of water pollution and were given the same textbooks to use. There is nothing factually wrong with Ben's homework, but Vanessa has produced a much more successful piece of work, because it is better organised and better presented.

For a start, Vanessa sticks to the subject – the causes of water pollution – while Ben's first paragraph is not directly relevant, dealing with the way we need and use water rather than with the causes of water pollution. As far as his second paragraph is concerned, Ben appears to have copied out some sentences from the books rather than tried to reorganise the information and put it into his own words. Vanessa, on the other hand, has used her reading and note-making skills to pick out the main causes of water pollution and to arrange the information in separate sections with headings and sub-headings.

●●● IN GROUPS ●●●

Study Vanessa's homework and discuss the use she makes of various note-making devices such as headings, numbers, underlining, capitals and brackets.

● ON YOUR OWN ●

Choose a piece of your homework and use the checklist (below) to check up on your presentation and organisation skills.

A Presentation

1 Did you put a date and a title, and underline them both?

2 Did you leave a margin?

3 Did you make sure that your handwriting was neat and that any crossings-out were done tidily?

4 Did you proofread the homework to check the punctuation and spelling before you handed it in?

5 Did you use a dictionary to check any spellings you were unsure of?

B Organisation

6 Was the work properly arranged in sections or paragraphs?

7 Did you make sure you used your own words rather than just copied out sentences from the textbook?

8 Did you make use of any of the following: sub-headings, underlining, numbers, capitals, brackets? If not, could you have done so?

9 Did you include enough details and/or examples to back up or illustrate the points you made?

10 Did you include any charts, diagrams or drawings? Would it have been useful to do so?

What are the strengths and weaknesses of a) the presentation b) the organisation of your homework? Set yourself targets for improvement. Write down one way in which you will try to improve the presentation and one way in which you will try to improve the organisation of your next piece of homework. Tell either a parent, a friend or a teacher what your targets for improvement are. Then, when you have done the homework, show it to them and discuss together how successful you have been at meeting your targets.

Title underlined ⟶ Vanessa Brown.

Causes of water pollution

11th May ⟵ *Date*

There are four main causes of the pollution of streams, rivers and lakes:

Use of sub-headings, underlined ⟶ Pollution from sewage
Usually only treated sewage is discharged. Untreated sewage (containing lots of bacteria) is discharged during heavy rains.
N.B. Liquid wastes are called effluents. ⟵

Use of brackets in which to put additional information

Use of numbers to distinguish different points ⟶ Pollution from industrial wastes.
1. Uncontrolled discharge of chemicals (e.g. cadmium) which kill living things.
2. Warm water from power stations. Reduces level of O_2 in water killing fish.
3. Fumes mix with rainwater, making ACID RAIN. Gets into rivers, lakes. Kills fish, plants.

Use of underlining and capitals to draw attention to technical terms

Agricultural pollution
1. Farmyard wastes (e.g. liquid manure — slurry) very poisonous (toxic).
2. Fertilizers (e.g. nitrates) washed out of soil into streams and rivers.
3. Pesticides. Washed out or may drift during spraying.

Use of examples

Pollution from household rubbish
Toxic wastes from landfill tips seep into rivers.

The main causes of sea pollution are:
sewage, toxic wastes, oil.

Water Pollution

Ben Jenkins

Water is vital to all life. An adult needs to drink two litres of water per day. People also use water for cooking and washing and in the manufacture of goods in factories.

Human activity causes pollution at every level of the water cycle. Each year thousands of tonnes of human sewage and poisonous chemicals are discharged into our streams, rivers and seas. The fertilisers and pesticides which farmers use also contribute to pollution because they get washed into streams, rivers and lakes. Water pollution causes damage to the environment and its natural life forms.

2 Finding information

USING THE LIBRARY OR RESOURCES CENTRE

When you need information on a topic, the most obvious place to look is the school or public library. As well as looking on the shelves to see if there is a book that is suitable for your needs, remember to look in the reference section for encyclopedias, and to check whether the library has any CD Roms, computer programs or audio-visual materials.

How to find a non-fiction book

Information books are known as non-fiction books and are kept in a section of the library known as the non-fiction section. Libraries use a system of numbers, known as a classification system, to help you to find the book you want.

Each book is given a classification number according to its subject and the number is put on the spine of the book. All the books on the same subject are stored in the same section of the library. So if you want a book on a particular subject, or if you know the number of a book, you can find out which shelf it is on by looking at a plan of the library.

There are various classification systems, but the one most commonly used is the Dewey Decimal System.

Each book is put into one of ten main classes. Each of these main classes is then divided into ten subjects. Each subject heading has its own number. In the example, the ten subject headings in the Science class are listed. Each of these subject headings are then broken down into ten more divisions. In the example, the ten divisions within the subject Physics have been listed. Books are placed in the most relevant classification and each one is numbered individually using decimal numbers after the subject division number.

All the books in the library are shelved according to their number, so books on a particular subject are all found in the same area of the library. Therefore, if you know the number of a subject or a particular book you can easily locate it in the library.

000 GENERAL	500 PURE SCIENCES	530 PHYSICS
100 PHILOSOPHY	510 MATHEMATICS	531 MECHANICS
200 RELIGION	520 ASTRONOMY	532 MECHANICS OF FLUIDS
300 SOCIAL SCIENCE	530 PHYSICS ⟶	533 MECHANICS OF GASES
400 LANGUAGES	540 CHEMISTRY	534 SOUND
500 PURE SCIENCE ⟶	550 PHYSICAL GEOGRAPHY	535 LIGHT
600 TECHNOLOGY (APPLIED SCIENCE)	560 PALAEOTOLOGY	536 HEAT
700 THE ARTS	570 BIOLOGY	537 ELECTRICITY & ELECTRONICS
800 LITERATURE	580 BOTANY	538 MAGNETISM
900 GEOGRAPHY/BIOGRAPHY/HISTORY	590 ZOOLOGY	539 MODERN PHYSICS

Using the catalogue

Details of all the books and other materials stored in the library are kept on a catalogue. If you are looking for a particular book or want to find out if a library has information on a particular subject, look in the catalogue.

There are several different types of catalogue. In many libraries, the catalogue is on computer. There is also usually a paper print-out of the catalogue. In some libraries, the catalogue is stored on microfilm or microfiches. Other libraries still use a card-index system in which details of the catalogue are stored on cards.

The catalogue is usually arranged in three parts:

1 **An author catalogue.** This is arranged alphabetically by author.

2 **A subject catalogue.** This is arranged by classification numbers and gives details of all the materials the library stocks on a particular subject.

3 **A subject index.** This is a list of subjects in alphabetical order (e.g. planets, plants, plastic) with the classification number for each subject. You can use the subject index to find out the number you need to look up in the subject catalogue to see if the library stocks any books on that subject. If you cannot find the subject you are looking for, it may be because it is listed under different name. Look up a word which is more general or a word which means the same or almost the same.

ON YOUR OWN

Carry out a catalogue search. Use the subject index to find the subject heading and the Dewey classification number for books on each of the following topics. (The first one has been done for you.)

1 Sound – *Physics 534*

2 Japan

3 Volcanoes

4 Forests

5 Immunisation

6 Textiles

7 Musical instruments

8 Monasteries

9 Air pollution

10 Hinduism

Now use the subject catalogue to find out which books the library stocks on any **two** of these topics. Write down the author and title of a book on each topic and look for them on the library shelves.

Finally, choose a topic which you are studying at present. Look it up in the subject index. Check in the subject catalogue to see if the library stocks any books on that topic. Note down the titles and look for them on the library shelves. Then check to see whether the library has any CD Roms which may contain information on your topic.

Finding information on farming

Finding Information Flow Chart
(The Oxford Children's Encyclopedia)

- Begin
- Do you know which shelves the farming books are on? — **NO** →
  - Is the librarian available to help? — **NO** →
    - Look up farming in the subject catalogue – find the Dewey number e.g. 630
  - **YES** ↓
    - Ask the librarian where the farming books are
  - **YES** ↓ (from first question)
  - Use the plan of the library to locate the shelves you need
- Go to the shelves where the farming books are kept
- Is there a suitable book on the shelves? — **NO** →
  - Do you need the information now? — **NO** →
    - Look in the Dewey catalogue or microfilm for the number you found earlier – choose a suitable sounding book
    - Go to the counter and reserve the book
  - **YES** ↓
    - Go to the reference section and check the encyclopedias for information instead
- **YES** ↓
  - Take it to the counter to get it stamped out
- End

Look at the flow diagram which shows how to find information on farming, to help you understand how to use the library system.

COLLECTING DATA

IN PAIRS

Study the diagram. Choose one of the investigations listed below and work out a project plan which explains what you want to find out, the questions you want to answer and the methods you are going to use to collect information.

Topics for investigation:

● What life was like in Britain during the Second World War.

● How industry has changed and developed in your local area over the past 150 years.

● The changing role and status of women in twentieth century Britain.

● How the building of new roads has affected the local area in the last 50 years.

In many subjects you will have to carry out investigations. You will have to learn how to collect and analyse data from various different sources. When you are planning an investigation, you need to think about how you are going to collect the information you need.

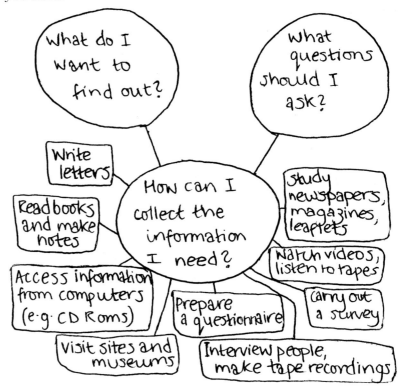

Interviews

Interviews are a useful source of information if you want to collect opinions as well as facts. Interviews would be ideal, for example, if you wanted not only to find out how something has changed over a period of time, but also how that change has affected people's lives.

PLANNING AND CONDUCTING AN INTERVIEW

Interviews are easier to arrange if you know the person:

● Write to them or phone them up

● Explain how long the interview would take (twenty minutes is usually long enough)

● Try to fit in with the date and time they can offer

● Prepare a list of questions

● If they don't mind; tape-record the interview

● Make detailed notes

● Stop now and then to summarise what has been said

● Thank the person

● Go through your notes and sum up the key points.

ON YOUR OWN

Practise your interviewing skills. Imagine that you are carrying out an investigation into how teenagers spent their leisure time in the past and how they spend it now. Plan and then conduct interviews with one or two adults you know about how teenagers' use of leisure time has changed. Then hold a class discussion in which you talk about how the interviews went and what you learned from the activity about **a)** how teenagers' leisure interests have changed **b)** how to plan and conduct interviews.

Measurements and Observations

A lot of information can be collected through either measurement or observation. For example, you can survey weather patterns by taking regular measurements of such things as rainfall and temperature; you can survey the types of building in a street by counting how many of each type there are; or you can study traffic patterns by counting the different types of vehicle which use a particular road at different times of the day.

Questionnaires

A questionnaire is a list of questions which can be used to find out facts about people, and their opinions on various issues. It provides structured information which you can analyse in order to draw conclusions.

PREPARING A QUESTIONNAIRE

There are two types of question you can ask:

1 **Closed questions.** The answer is restricted to one of a list of choices.
   e.g. What sort of school do you go to? Mixed, Single-sex
   Do you enjoy English lessons? Always, Sometimes, Never

2 **Open-ended questions.** No choices are given and therefore there is no restriction on the answer.
   e.g. Which sport(s) do you like watching on TV?

The advantage of closed questions is that they provide data which is easy to analyse.

The advantage of open-ended questions is that people are not forced to choose between your alternatives, but can choose the answer for themselves which means it is more accurate.

Sometimes, with closed questions, people find that none of the suggested answers is relevant to them. This problem can be overcome by including the choice *'other' (please specify)* and a space for an answer to be written. This is a compromise between closed and open questions.

∞∞ IN PAIRS ∞∞

Study the questionnaire which Donna drew up in order to investigate pupils' use of her local leisure centre. Discuss what she will learn about the use of the leisure centre from the questions she asks. What conclusions do you think she will be able to draw from the answers she gets?

Plan and produce a questionnaire to find out about the holiday patterns of people in your school. After you have drawn up your questionnaire, form a group with two other pairs, compare your questionnaires and discuss how you might improve them.

Pupils' use of Hamley Leisure Centre

Interviewer: Donna Marks   *Date:* 11 January 1996

1 **Sex**   male ❑   female ❑

2 **Age**   11/12 ❑   13/14 ❑
             15/16 ❑   17/18 ❑

3 **How often do you visit the leisure centre?**
   more than once a week ❑   once a week ❑
   once a month ❑   less than once a month ❑
   never ❑

4 **How far away from the leisure centre do you live?**
   Under a mile ❑   1-3 miles ❑
   4-6 miles ❑   over 6 miles ❑

5 **Do you visit the leisure centre**
   on you own ❑   with your family ❑
   with your friends ❑

6 **Which of these activities have you done at the leisure centre in the last 6 months?**
   swimming ❑   aerobics ❑   badminton ❑
   weight-training ❑   judo ❑   table-tennis ❑
   other (please specify) _____

7 **What is your main reason for visiting the leisure centre?**
   _____

8 **State one way in which you think facilities at the leisure centre could be improved?**
   _____

3 Understanding information

DEVELOPING YOUR READING SKILLS

There are many ways of reading a passage to gather information. The method you use will depend on the purpose of your reading and the type of material you are reading.

There are three main methods you can use:

1 SKIMMING. You read quickly, not trying to take in all the details, in order to get a general idea of what a passage or article is about or to find out what information a book contains. If you are skimming through a book you will look at such things as the contents, headings, introductions and conclusions. Your aim is to find out whether the book will provide the information you need. Similarly, if you are skimming through a passage, you won't try to take in everything it says at once. Your aim is to find out whether the passage interests you and contains the information you are searching for.

2 SCANNING. You run your eye quickly down the page, not trying to read every sentence, searching for the sentence or paragraph that will give you a particular piece of information. Scanning is a useful method to use when you want to check an important point, such as a date or the meaning of a technical term, or to extract some particular details from a passage.

3 CLOSE READING. You read a chapter, passage or article carefully, studying it in detail in order to obtain as much information as possible from it. Your aim is to try to understand all the facts and ideas it contains, so you may read it several times and take notes in order to help you to remember what you have read.

ON YOUR OWN

● Skim through the passage at the top of page 19 quickly once to find out which of the following six subjects it contains information about: Jewish religious festivals; The synagogue; Jewish family prayers; Jewish initiation ceremonies; The Jewish Sabbath; Jewish sacred texts.

● Now scan through the passage in order to find out a) what a kippah is b) what hallah is.

● Read the passage closely to discover what is distinctive about Jewish praying. List six key facts you learn about Jewish praying.

IN GROUPS

Compare your lists and draw up a list of the six most important facts you learn from the passage.

IN PAIRS

Go through the passage again and make a list of words that are connected with Jewish praying. Work out what each word means and draw up a glossary, listing the words in alphabetical order together with their meanings.

More Jewish worship takes place in the home than in the synagogue. Within the family circle prayers are said three times a day – morning, afternoon and evening. On each weekday morning a Jewish man puts on his tefillin. These are small leather boxes with extracts from the scriptures in them, which are attached to the body with leather straps. He fixes one around his forehead to show that he is thinking about God and one on his left arm, close to his heart, to show that he loves God. He then places a small skull-cap or kippah upon his head and puts a shawl, called a tallit, around his shoulders.

At sunset on a Friday evening the Sabbath Day begins in the home when the mother of the family lights candles and prays:

> Blessed are you, O Lord our God, ruler of the universe who makes us holy by doing your commands and has commanded us to light the Sabbath Candle.

The father says the Kiddush. This traditional prayer, usually sung over a glass of wine, is a symbol of happiness and joy. It includes the blessing:

> Blessed art thou, O Lord our God, King of the universe, who creates the fruit of the vine.

The freshly baked bread sitting on the table in the form of two specially plaited loaves is called hallah [plural: hallot]. God provided the Israelites with a mysterious food called manna in the wilderness when they had nothing to eat and on the day before the Sabbath Moses told them to collect a double portion. After the ceremonial washing of hands, which is always done before eating bread, the loaves are blessed and God is thanked for providing all things:

> Blessed art thou, O God, King of the universe, who brings forth bread out of the earth.

The Sabbath ends on Saturday after sunset with prayers of thanksgiving to God. This time the special prayer is the Havdalah. A plaited candle is lit to symbolise the return to work and a spice box is passed round the family so that everyone can smell the fragrance of its contents. The prayer is that the fragrance of this Sabbath Day will continue through all of the week to come.

(adapted from *New Steps in Religious Education Book 1* by Michael Keene)

Interpreting the evidence

When you read texts closely in a subject such as history, you have to develop the skill of interpreting the text in order to understand the point of view of the person who is describing the events.

IN PAIRS

Here are two different views of the dropping of the atom bomb on Hiroshima in the Second World War. Study the extracts closely and discuss the different interpretations of the event that the two accounts give.

Extract A *The Hiroshima bomb, 6 August 1945*

Suddenly a glaring light appeared in the sky accompanied by an unnatural tremor and a wave of suffocating heat and a wind which swept away everything in its path... thousands in the streets scorched by the searing heat... others screaming in agony from the pain of their burns. Everything standing upright was annihilated and the debris carried up into the air... trams, trains... flung like toys. About half an hour after, a fine rain began to fall caused by the sudden rise of over-heated air to a great height where it condensed. Then a violent wind rose and the fire extended with terrible rapidity. There was nothing left to burn, Hiroshima had ceased to exist.

(from *Warrior without weapons* M.Junod)

Extract B
The bombing of Hiroshima

If the atom bombs had not been dropped the War would have dragged on. Those terrible bombs must have seemed as supernatural to the Japanese as they seemed to me when I first heard of them in the darkness and danger of our own prison. For me, selfish as it may sound, there was the certain knowledge that if the bomb had not been dropped, the Japanese would have fought on, and hundreds of thousands of prisoners would have been killed. Even if we had not been massacred, we were near our physical end through lack of food.

(from *Night of the New Moon* by I. van der Post, 1970)

PRACTISE YOUR READING SKILLS

•• IN PAIRS ••

Skim the article about Barbados, which is taken from an encyclopedia, to find out what the article is about.

● Which of these four statements is the most accurate summary of what the article is about?

1 The article gives detailed information about the people of Barbados and describes their homes, their jobs, the clothes they wear and the food they eat.

2 The article describes present-day Barbados, compares it with other West Indian islands and explains what its future development is likely to be.

3 The article gives the main facts about present-day Barbados, explains its geographical features and gives details of the island's historical past.

4 The article explains why tourism has become an important industry in Barbados and gives details of the island's main tourist attractions and leisure facilities.

● Scan through the article and find the paragraphs which give you information about Barbados's exports and imports.

● ON YOUR OWN ●

● Read the article closely. Then copy out and complete these sentences by choosing the correct endings.

1 In the group of islands called the West Indies, Barbados is
   a) the most easterly   **b)** the most westerly.

2 The weather in Barbados is
   a) very hot, because it lies in the tropics
   b) not too hot, because of the cool trade winds.

3 It was named Barbados after
   a) the coral reefs around the island
   b) the fig trees growing on the island.

4 For an island of its size Barbados has
   a) a large population   **b)** a small population.

5 Barbados has
   a) a lot of mineral resources   **b)** no mineral resources except oil.

6 Most of its foodstuffs are
   a) grown on the island   **b)** imported.

7 The national sport in Barbados is
   a) cricket   **b)** football.

8 The first Europeans to settle in Barbados were
   a) English   **b)** Portuguese.

9 The capital of Barbados is
   a) Kingston   **b)** Bridgetown.

10 The island of Barbados is
   a) an independent Commonwealth country
   b) a British colony.

•• IN PAIRS ••

● The article on Barbados is about 450 words long. Write an article on Barbados that is only 150 words long. Before writing anything, go through the article and discuss what to keep in and what to leave out. Compare your shortened version of the article with those of other pairs. Discuss which is best and why.

● Study the table of *Facts About Barbados* that is included in the article. Then, scan through the article about Jamaica (right), pick out the necessary details, and produce a similar factbox about Jamaica.

Barbados

BARBADOS, is the most easterly island in the West Indies. It is bordered by the Atlantic Ocean on the east and the Caribbean Sea to the west. Roughly triangular in shape, the island extends 34 kilometres (21 miles) from north to south and 22 kilometres (14 miles) from east to west.

For part of the year Barbados enjoys the cool northeast trade winds and this helps to explain why, although it is in the tropics, the weather is not too hot. The island is almost encircled with coral reefs and its highest point, mount Hillaby in the north central region, is no more than 337 metres (1,105 feet) above the sea. Early Portuguese explorers named the island Barbados, meaning 'bearded', after the fig trees there which looked like beards.

In spite of its small size Barbados has about 252,700 people, which is more than can comfortably make a living from the island. Over 90 per cent of the people are descended from Africans who were brought as slaves from West Africa in the 17th and 18th centuries. Many earn their living from the sugar industry, either growing and harvesting the cane or manufacturing it into sugar, molasses (syrup), or rum. Tourism is an important industry as is fishing.

There is known to be oil beneath the ground but Barbados has no other mineral resources. Nearly all the original forest was cleared so that sugar-cane could be planted and Barbados now has to import timber. It also has to import most of its foodstuffs.

Barbadians are well known for their Calypso music and the steel bands which play it. Cricket is their national sport and Barbados has produced many famous cricketers.

History

The Portuguese were among the first Europeans to sight the island in the 16th century, but the English were the first settlers. When they arrived in 1625 the island had long been abandoned by the original native Indian inhabitants. The English imported slaves fom West Africa to work on their sugar plantations and their numbers grew rapidly. Slavery was abolished in 1834, but sugar continued to dominate the economy.

Among their ancient institutions Barbadians are especially proud of Codrington College, founded in 1710, the oldest centre of higher education in the West Indies. The capital of Barbados is Bridgetown, founded in 1628, and this is also the only port. It has a deep-water harbour. Bridgetown has a population of about 7,500.

In 1966, Barbados ceased to be a colony of Great Britain and became an independent country and member of the Commonwealth, with the queen of England as head of state. The government is led by the prime minister. The parliament of Barbados consists of the Senate and the House of Assembly, and the Queen is represented by a governor-general.

FACTS ABOUT BARBADOS

AREA: 430 square kilometres (166 square miles)
POPULATION: 252,700
KIND OF COUNTRY: Independent parliamentary state; member of the Commonwealth of Nations.
CAPITAL: Bridgetown
GEOGRAPHICAL FEATURES: An island with a gently hilly landscape, its coast almost encircled by coral reefs.
LEADING INDUSTRIES: Sugar, molasses, rum, tourism.

(adapted from the *Children's Britannica*)

JAMAICA is the largest English-speaking island in the Caribbean with an area of 10,991 square kilometres (4,244 square miles). It became an independent country in 1962 and is a member of the Commonwealth.

Jamaica is a very varied country. Much of the interior is mountainous and sparsely populated. Kingston, the capital, is a crowded modern city, but only a few kilometres away are the Blue Mountains, covered in forests, where the highest peak rises to 2,256 metres (7,400 feet). Elsewhere there are huge swamps, dry hills, and prosperous farms on the fertile plains between the hills and the shore.

There are also sharp contrasts between great wealth and extreme poverty. The population is 2,355,100. Most Jamaicans are descended from African slaves who were brought to the island in the 17th and 18th centuries to grow sugar cane. Much of the best land is still owned by big sugar estates. Factories process the cane to make sugar for export. There are also estates growing bananas, vegetables and other crops; and there are many small farmers who grow vegetables and fruits and keep animals. Jamaican Blue Mountain coffee is probably the best in the world.

Jamaica is also one of the world's leading producers of bauxite. This is a red clay, which is exported to other countries and processed to get aluminium. There are also many factories on the island. Some make goods which can be sold locally. Others stitch clothing or assemble goods for export to the USA.

Many tourists visit Jamaica. The main tourist resorts are Ocho Rios and Montego Bay on the north coast. There are fine sandy beaches for swimming and water sports, and beautiful tropical mountain scenery.

(adapted from *The Oxford Children's Encyclopedia*)

UNDERSTANDING CHARTS AND GRAPHS

Information is sometimes provided in the form of charts or graphs where it is easy to understand at a glance. It is important for you to learn how to interpret data which is presented in this way, and to be able to produce your own charts and graphs.

Pie charts

A pie chart looks like a pie which has been cut into slices. Pie charts are used to show the proportions of a set of figures.

ON YOUR OWN

What do you learn, from Figure 1, about the main sources of salt in our diets? Use the information from the pie chart, in Figure 1, to suggest two things you should do if you want to reduce the amount of salt in your diet.

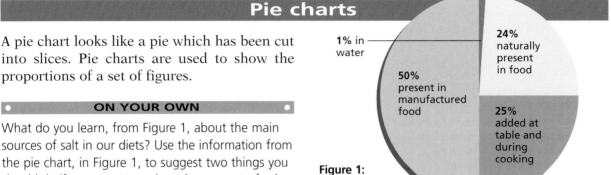

Figure 1: Sources of salt in our diet

Bar charts

A bar chart can be used to show the same sort of information as a pie chart. They can be used when you have a set of data which does not make a whole – for example, only some of the components which make up a budget. For a pie chart, a whole set of data is required because the chart represents the whole, split into proportions.

However, sometimes a whole set of data is presented better in a bar chart than a pie chart because there are several pieces of information. A pie chart with too many segments can become confusing, especially if several of the segments are very small.

A bar chart can also be used to show and compare measurements which change over time. Figure 2 shows you the average amount of rainfall and hours of sunshine in Montego Bay, Jamaica, for each month of the year.

ON YOUR OWN

Study the information given in Figure 2, then write a short paragraph saying what you have learned from it about the pattern of weather throughout the year, and what you think the main tourist season in Montego Bay is likely to be.

Figure 2: The climate of Montego Bay, Jamaica

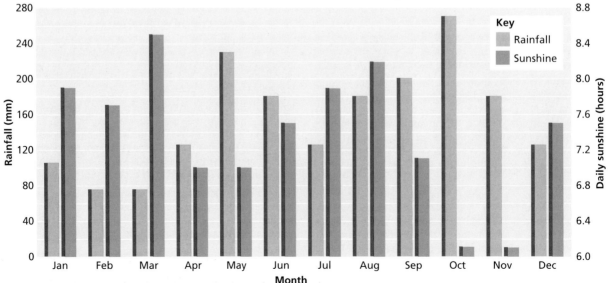

Pictograms

A pictogram is similar to a bar chart. Instead of bars or blocks, appropriate symbols are used. Figure 3 is a pictogram showing the number of cars that travelled along a road on a Monday.

•• IN PAIRS ••

Why do you think there were more cars between the hours of **a)** 7am – 9am **b)** 3pm – 5pm **c)** 5pm – 7pm?

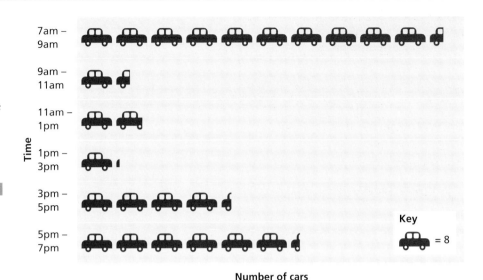

Figure 3: Number of cars, Monday 7am – 7pm

Line graphs

A line graph is another way of showing measurements which change over time. It can be used to show two or more sets of data. In Figure 4 there are two sets of data, providing information on the birth rate and the death rate during a seventy-year period in Bangladesh. Figure 5 shows the trends in the total population of Bangladesh over the same seventy-year period between 1921-1991.

•• IN PAIRS ••

Study Figures 4 and 5 and answer these questions.

1 What do you learn about the trends in **a)** the birth rate **b)** the death rate in Bangladesh between 1921 and 1991?

2 What has happened to the total population in Bangladesh between 1921 and 1991?

3 Explain why the population of Bangladesh increased very rapidly between 1921 and 1991.

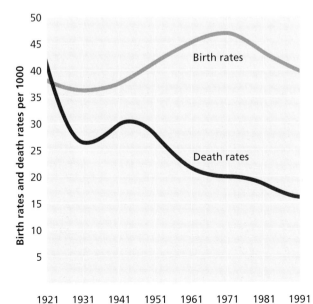

Figure 4: Bangladesh 1921-91, birth and death rates

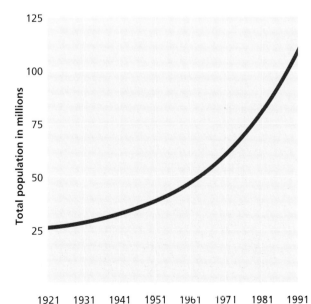

Figure 5: Bangladesh 1921-91, total population

4 Notes and notemaking

MAKING NOTES

•• IN PAIRS ••

Read Passage A. It explains what the United Nations is, who belongs to it, how it is organised, and what the General Assembly is. Then study the two sets of notes on the passage – Example 1 and Example 2.

Talk about the different techniques which the notemakers have used. Discuss how in Example 1 numbers and headings are used to divide the notes into separate sections. Notes like this are sometimes called 'block notes'.

Discuss how in Example 2 the notes are arranged in the form of a 'spider diagram' or 'spidergram'. Each main leg of the spidergram deals with a separate part of the topic, with lines branching out from each leg to give further details. Talk about which set of notes you find easier to understand, and discuss why.

Passage A

It is important to develop your notemaking skills, because they will help you to learn from your reading. Reading a passage closely in order to make notes can help you to understand the text more fully. The notes also serve as a record, which you can use to help you remember what you have read.

Before you start making notes, you must always be clear about what information you want to extract from the text. You need to think about which pieces of information in the text are relevant to the particular aspect of the topic which you are studying. There are also various different notemaking techniques you can use, so you need to decide which type of notes you are going to make.

UNITED NATIONS

The United Nations (often known simply as the UN) is an organisation of more than 160 countries that have, of their own free will, decided to work for world peace and the maintenance of international security. It was set up officially on 24 October 1945, at the end of World War II.

The constitution of the United Nations, that is, the way in which it is organised, is known as the UN Charter. It sets out the purposes of the United Nations, which can be described as follows: to prevent war; to promote human rights; to encourage nations to respect international agreements; and to help all people have a better standard and quality of life. The UN also works for the improvement of conditions for the poor, to combat disease and to bring education to millions who cannot read and write.

To become a member of the United Nations, a country must say it wants peace, be willing to accept the aims of the UN Charter, and be judged by the UN as able to carry out these aims. The Security Council recommends new members and the General Assembly confirms the recommendation. There were 51 original members of the UN. Now there are more than 160, many of them ex-colonies which have become independent. Some of these newer states are very small, but all UN members have equal voting powers, regardless of size. So the original members have less power than formerly.

The United Nations is divided into six main working groups. These are the General Assembly, the Security Council, the Economic and Social Council, the Trusteeship Council, the International Court of Justice, and the Secretariat. The headquarters of the Secretariat is in New York. Most of the other groups usually meet in New York or Geneva in Switzerland, but the International Court sits at The Hague in the Netherlands. Meetings on specialised topics, such as drug abuse or the environment, often take place at UN offices in Vienna (Austria), Nairobi (Kenya), or other regional headquarters.

General Assembly. This is the main body of the UN and meets once a year. Sometimes it holds special or emergency meetings. All UN members are represented in the General Assembly and each has only one vote, whether it is a large country or a small one. The Assembly is rather like a parliament and delegates express their views on world problems.

When an important question has to be settled by the General Assembly, such as one concerning the admission of a new member, at least two-thirds of the members must be in favour.

Example 1

United Nations (U.N. Set up Oct 1945)

1. **Membership** Over 160 countries. Original no. 51. Some new states v. small. Equal voting power regardless of size.

2. **Aims** Set out in U.N. Charter:
   - prevent war
   - promote human rights
   - encourage nations to keep international agreements
   - improve standard and quality of life
   - help poor
   - combat disease
   - develop education for all

3. **Organisation** 6 main groups. General Assembly, Security council, Economic and Social Council, International Court of Justice, Secretariat (H.Q. New York)

4. **General Assembly** Meets once a year. Similar to a parliament. Each country has 1 vote. Important issues (e.g. admission of a new member) must have two thirds in favour.

Example 2

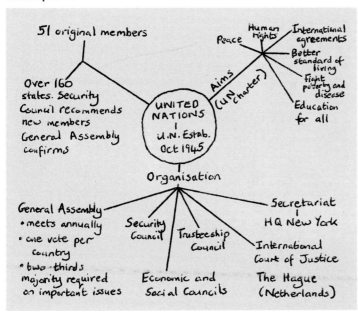

Passage B

Security Council. This is chiefly responsible for international peace and security, and consists of 15 members. Five of them (the United States, Great Britain, France, the Russian Federation, and China) always form part of the Security Council and are known as permanent members. The ten other members each serve for two years after being elected to the Security Council by the General Assembly.

Because the quarrels which come before the Security Council are generally political ones, the 15 nations do not always agree on a settlement. When they are voting to reach a decision any of the 15 members can say 'no'. When one of the permanent members says 'no', this is known as a *veto*. The Security Council can take action only when nine of its members, including all the permanent ones, say 'yes', although permanent members may abstain from voting without blocking action by the council. However, there are other ways in which the United Nations can act. For example, the General Assembly can be summoned for an emergency session to deal with a crisis.

When there is a dispute between nations, the Security Council may investigate it and call upon the nations to settle it peacefully. If this does not happen the Council may suggest ways of settling the dispute. If fighting has actually started, the Security Council may call for a cease-fire or for the cutting off of trade and all rail, sea, postal, air, and other means of communication. United Nations officials try to arrange peace talks. If a cease-fire is arranged, a UN peace-keeping force, consisting of troops from member countries, may be sent to the trouble spot.

ON YOUR OWN

Read Passage B, which explains what the Security Council is and what it does. Then, make a set of notes to add either to Example 1 or Example 2.

IN GROUPS

Compare your notes with those which other people have made. Decide who has made the best notes and discuss why.

PRACTISE YOUR NOTEMAKING SKILLS

An important skill you need to develop when you are making notes is the ability to pick out the key facts and ideas from a passage. Before you start making your notes, always remind yourself of the questions you are trying to answer. Then, as you make your notes, concentrate on choosing the information that is relevant to those questions.

ON YOUR OWN

Passage C is an extract from a textbook article on the European Union. It contains information on the membership of the European Union, its institutions, its aims and its historical development.

First, skim read the article and decide which paragraph or paragraphs tell you about **a)** its membership **b)** its aims **c)** its institutions **d)** its historical development.

Then, make notes in answer to these questions.

1 When and why was the European Economic Community set up?

2 How has the European Union changed in the past forty years?

3 How is the European Union organised?

IN GROUPS

Compare your notes with those other people have made. Who do you think has made the best notes? Discuss why.

Passage C

THE EUROPEAN UNION

The European Union (EU) is a group of 15 Member States committed to the development of economic and political cooperation. The Union aims to bring the peoples of Europe closer together by breaking down the economic and political barriers which have traditionally divided Europe, and to promote peace and prosperity for its 344 million members.

The European Union developed in the aftermath of the Second World War. In 1957, Italy, France, West Germany, Belgium, the Netherlands and Luxembourg signed the Treaty of Rome, setting up the European Economic Community. The EEC, or Common Market, as it became known, came into operation in 1958. Since then, a further nine countries have joined. The expansion began in 1973 with the addition of the United Kingdom, Ireland and Denmark. Greece joined in 1981, followed by Spain and Portugal in 1986. When Germany was unified in 1990, the 18 million citizens of the former East Germany automatically became members. The most recent states to join are Austria, Finland and Sweden in 1995. The EEC was renamed the European Community (EC) in 1965, and changed its name to the European Union in 1992.

The main decision-making body of the EU is the Council of Ministers. It consists of government ministers from each of the Member States. The participating ministers vary according to the topic under discussion e.g. foreign affairs, agriculture, transport.

The Council acts mainly on proposals from the European Commission, which has its headquarters in Brussels. The Commission is responsible for planning and implementing European law. The 20 members of the Commission are nominated by national governments, but are bound by oath to act independently in the interests of the Community as a whole.

Before the Council can take a final decision, proposed legislation has to be scrutinised by the European Parliament. In certain areas, the Parliament and the Council make joint decisions. There are 626 members of the European Parliament, who are elected every five years. Germany has 99 members and France, the United Kingdom and Italy all have 87 members. Smaller states have seats broadly in accordance with the size of their population e.g. Finland and Denmark have 16, Luxembourg has 6.

Study passage D. It explains the process whereby iron ore is smelted in a blast furnace in order to remove impurities and to produce iron, which can be used to make steel. Read the passage and then work together to produce **a)** a set of notes in the form of a diagram **b)** a set of block notes arranged as numbered points.

Discuss which type of notes **a)** was easier to produce **b)** was most useful in helping you to understand the process **c)** would be easier to revise from.

Passage D

Smelting Iron

Iron ore contains sand, clay, and water as impurities, together with other elements such as phosphorus and sulphur which are disadvantageous in steel and so must be removed.

Iron is separated from the ore by smelting in a blast furnace. The blast furnace is a very large steel tube, or stack, set on end and lined with fire-resisting bricks. The stack is fed continuously with a carefully blended mixture of ore, coke, and limestone, some of which has been heated together previously to form a clinker or 'sinter'.

Near the bottom of the furnace hot air is blown in through a pipe and a number of nozzles called *tuyères*. The coke burns fiercely as the hot air passes up through the 'burden' combining with oxygen to form carbon monoxide which removes the oxygen from the iron ore. As the oxygen is removed, the iron melts and trickles down to collect in the bottom of the furnace as a molten pool on the hearth. The limestone 'fluxes' the sand, clay, and other earthy impurities from the charge by reacting with them to form a liquid slag which floats on top of the iron in the hearth. It can also react with sulphur and phosphorus and remove a large proportion of these harmful elements.

The hot gases produced at the bottom of the furnace pass upwards through the stack. The gas (coal gas) emerging from the top of the stack is useful. It is hot and contains carbon monoxide which can be burnt to heat the ingoing air blast, to generate steam power for blowing or pumping the air blast, and in some plants to generate electricity.

About every five hours molten iron is 'tapped' or run through a tap hole into ladles or conveying vessels. It is then transferred either to steel-making furnaces in its liquid form, or to pig-casting machines where the molten iron is poured into moulds to make small blocks called 'pigs'. Slag is trapped approximately every two hours through a hole a little highter than the tap hole. Blast furnace slag is a useful by-product. It can be used for roadstone and railway ballast, some is 'foamed' with steam for brickmaking, and some is granulated for cement manufacture.

5 Developing your writing skills

A STEP-BY-STEP APPROACH TO WRITING

Many pupils find writing tasks difficult because they do not adopt a structured approach to their writing. The step-by-step approach shown below can help you to organise and develop your writing in all your subjects.

STEP 1 – DEFINING YOUR PURPOSE AND AUDIENCE

What is the purpose of your writing? Are you trying to tell a story? To describe a personal experience? To report your observations? To explain a process? To convey factual information or instructions on a particular topic? To express your opinion? To develop an argument?

Before you begin a writing task, think about the purpose of the writing and make sure you are clear what the task requires you to do.

Who is going to read your writing? What audience are you aiming at? You need to make sure you understand who your audience is because it will affect the way you write. For example, you will structure and organise your writing differently if you are writing to explain something for an examiner in an essay from the way you will write on a similar topic for a newspaper or magazine article, or in a letter to a friend.

STEP 2 – COLLECTING INFORMATION AND IDEAS

Once you have defined the purpose and audience of your writing, the next step is to think about what information and ideas you might include. Look at any notes you have already made on the subject and do a brainstorm - listing all the information and ideas that you might possibly include. Put down everything that might possibly be useful. It's better at this stage to have too much rather than too little. Don't worry about putting it in any particular order – you can do that at the planning stage (see below).

Here is the brainstorm Sophie did when thinking about what to include in an article on smoking:

STEP 3 — PLANNING

Once you have brainstormed about what you might include, you need to select the key ideas and work out a plan which puts them in the most logical order. Some people do this by writing numbers beside each point on the same piece of paper. Others, like Sophie, prefer to write their plan out as a flow chart (see below).

In addition to deciding on an order for the main points, you need to think of a good way of starting (an introduction) and a good way of finishing (a conclusion). Don't feel that it is absolutely necessary to include everything from your brainstorm in your plan. There may be some ideas which you reject at the planning stage, either because they do not fit or because you have been asked to write only a certain number of words and you won't have space for all your ideas.

Title - why I can't stand smoking.

↓

Introduction - my views - it's dirty, antisocial and dangerous.

↓

Para 2 - the health risks

↓

Para 3 - it's antisocial. Dangers of passive smoking.

↓

Para 4 - it's dirty. Clothes, teeth, breath, stains, ashtrays.

↓

Para 5 - it's expensive and a waste of money.

↓

Conclusion - changes I'd like -
Ban all advertising,
Ban smoking in public places,
Charge medical fees for smoking related illnesses

STEP 4 — DRAFTING

Once you have made a plan, you can write your first draft. Don't worry if you have to cross things out or if you find that the sentences don't come out in quite the right order. Use arrows and asterisks to indicate where they should go. Also, don't worry at this stage if you are unsure about how to spell particular words - you can look up spellings later. What matters at this stage is the content of what you are writing so, if you suddenly think of something vitally important while you are writing, don't reject the idea because it wasn't in your original plan. Work out where it would fit in best and include it.

STEP 5 — REVISING AND REDRAFTING

When you have finished your first draft, do not try to revise and redraft it immediately.. Leave it for at least half-an-hour, then go back to it and think carefully about the content, structure and organisation.

Have you omitted any key points? If you have missed out something important where should it go in?

Are the points in the right order? Does it flow logically from one point to another?

Does the writing have a good start? Is there any way you could make it have a greater impact by making the start more punchy?

How does the writing end? Is the ending too abrupt? Does it need some sort of summary or conclusion?

Think carefully about the language you have used. Are there any sentences that need revising because you have not expressed the idea clearly enough? Is your language varied enough? Are there some places where you have repeated the same phrase too often? What alternatives could you have used? (If you can't think of any, use a thesaurus to help you.)

Is the style you have used appropriate for the purpose and audience? For example, if it is a formal piece of writing, have you included any slang expressions (e.g. 'at the end of the day') that are inappropriate?

STEP 6 – PROOFREADING

Before you produce your final neat copy of your writing, check it through to make sure that it is properly punctuated and correctly spelt (see pages 32–35).

STEP 7 – PRODUCING THE FINAL COPY

Produce the final neat copy, taking care with your handwriting to make sure that it is legible.

Note: Steps 4–7 can be done on a word processor (see page 39). There are many advantages in learning to draft on a word processor. For example, you can make changes more easily than if you are writing by hand. Also, once you have completed the drafting and proofreading, it is easy to print out as many copies as you require.

Practise your writing skills

Helen Campbell   1st December

Say what you think
The abuse of animals

A lot of the time animals are used to be tested on, many of them die. I dont think it fair that they ~~shot~~ should be treated in this way because they have just as many rights as people. Animals are often killed for food I dont like it but I still eat meat, but many are killed for their fur. I think this is horrible because we dont have to wear fur, some people only wear it to show off.

Some Animals like birds are chocked to death if there is an oil leakage, because they drink it.
Some people force feed animals to make them fat and ready to kill I dont think that animals should be made to eat ~~beaaus~~ because you wouldn't do that to a person.

At Christmas time many animals are neglected. Lots of people get them for christmas after a few months the ~~novatly~~ novalty ~~wheres off~~ wears off and ~~they throw~~ them out some are killed by cars.

People dont take as much care as they should do with animals, and If they did a lot more animals ~~would~~ wouldnt be killed.

IN PAIRS

Study Helen's piece of writing about the abuse of animals. She has lots of points to make about the abuse of animals, but the writing is not as well structured as it could have been because she didn't have a clear plan and she handed in her first draft, instead of redrafting it.

Using Helen's ideas, produce a plan that she might have drawn up, putting the ideas in a logical order, linking similar ideas in the same paragraph and putting separate ideas in separate paragraphs.

ON YOUR OWN

Revise and redraft Helen's writing using your plan. You will probably have to think of ways of developing some of her ideas more fully. Try to think of an interesting way of starting so that your first paragraph grabs the reader's attention.

IN CLASS

Compare your revised versions of Helen's essay in a class discussion. Decide whose works best and why.

ON YOUR OWN

Use the step-by-step approach to plan, draft and redraft an article for people of your own age, saying what you think about one of these topics:

● The way adults treat children

● Gambling

● What makes a good teacher

● Prejudice and discrimination

Writing in Geography and History

The step-by-step approach (see pages 28–30) can be used to help you to plan and write essays in subjects, such as history and geography. The following geography essay was written by Quincy Whitaker (13).

Feeding the World's Population

So far human ingenuity has coped with the problems caused by human population growth. Will this always be so?

Experiments have shown that when normally peaceful rats are kept in cramped, overcrowded conditions they become aggressive and dominant males appear. Although sociologists may argue about the comparison between humans and a cage full of rats, there are, nonetheless, lessons to be learnt from the experiment. Its results can, in some cases, be applied to today's society and the pressures which population growth has put on it. The increase in urban violence, for instance, can perhaps be linked with the problems of overcrowding which most inner-city areas face.

The increase in population has brought other problems as well as lack of space.

12% of the world population are starving and yet, overall, there is enough food in the world to feed everyone. There always has been and there will continue to be for quite some time. World population is increasing at a rapid rate, but with it people's knowledge of farming methods and synthetic and alternative sources of protein (soya and certain seafoods) are also growing. The amount of food which is produced in the world increases each year.

Although the population 'explosion' has contributed, it is not the main reason why 500,000,000 people are living below the starvation line.

The problem occurs in the division of the world's food supplies. One third of the world population lives in the richer countries of the North (that is America, Canada, Europe and Australasia) and yet we consume more than half the amount of cereals which are produced.

If human ingenuity is to begin to cope with the problems which confront it, then world wealth and therefore food supplies (or vice versa) will have to be redistributed via aid to the poorer countries in our world.

Meat is an extremely expensive and uneconomical method of taking in protein; more food would be produced if the land which is used for animal grazing was planted with cereal crops. If people in both the first and third worlds can be encouraged to obtain their protein from sources other than meat, such as beans, lentils, soya and seafood, then more cereal foods will be available worldwide.

Will human ingenuity always be able to cope with the problem of population growth? Technically, we are coping and will continue to cope. It is no longer a question of whether our ingenuity is capable, as it has proved to be so. It is a question of whether the rich countries of our world are far sighted enough to realise that it is to their own benefit (never mind that of the poorer countries) to lower their own living standards in return for the growth of the living standards of others.

It is in our interest to do this because when people face being hungry every day and homeless every month, the prospect of death can sometimes appear to be preferable to that of life. People become more willing to die for causes they believe in when life is no longer considered precious. A country will then face political instability and lose its investment potential. In the extreme, there is the possibility of war.

The decision to save 500,000,000 people from starvation rests with those who have political strength. Whether they choose to use their power cannot be predicted.

Quincy Whitaker

IN PAIRS

Produce a flow-chart showing how Quincy planned the development of the ideas through the essay.

Discuss how Quincy begins and ends the essay. Do you think the beginning and ending are effective? Can you suggest any alternative ways of beginning or ending the essay?

ON YOUR OWN

When you next have to write an essay in history or geography, make sure you use the step-by-step approach. After you have drawn up a plan, show it to either a friend or an adult and discuss it with them. You could ask for their suggestions at the revising and redrafting stage too.

PROOFREADING

Proofreading means checking your work to make sure that you have written what you intended to write, that the result is punctuated correctly and that there are no spelling mistakes. If your work is not punctuated properly and spelt correctly then the reader may not be able to understand what you have written. Anyone can make a careless error, so it is always important to proofread your work before you hand it in.

Developing your punctuation skills

WRITING COMPLETE SENTENCES

It is important to check that you have written complete sentences and capital letters and full stops correctly at the beginnings and ends of sentences. A sentence is a sequence of words capable of standing alone to make a statement, ask a question or give a command. It must begin with a capital letter and end with either a full stop, question mark or exclamation mark.

In the piece of writing (below), Katrina has plenty of ideas, but she has not structured and punctuated her sentences properly.

ON YOUR OWN

Study Katrina's piece of writing. Notice where she has not structured her sentences properly, and then decide how she might have divided it into paragraphs. Then copy it out in paragraphs, correcting it where she has not written proper sentences, and putting in capital letters and full stops at the beginning and end of each sentence.

IN GROUPS

When you have finished compare your version with those of other people.

KATRINA LEVINE   what makes a good   7/1/96
                           parent?

A good parent has to be able to understand all your problems, be kind and helpful in any way. they also must be able to cook. and wash. must be there when you're hart yourself. or your in trouble and not just turn you away. and be at your side when you are ill. they must be proud of you're ways. parents must take notice in your work. and buy you new clothes. not when you need it. but they must not spoil you to much. they must be kind at christmas and on your birthday. they must take you out and go places with you because you may need to get out. they must not coock the same meals all the time because you'll get sick of it.

USING PARAGRAPHS

It is also important to learn to paragraph your work properly. A paragraph is a group of sentences, all of which deal with the same theme or topic, or with one particular feature of a theme or topic. Writers start new paragraphs to help their readers understand that they are going to write about another feature of a topic or to introduce an entirely new topic. To show us where a new paragraph begins, writers do two things:

- start the first sentence of a new paragraph on a new line;
- leave a space between the margin and the first words of a new paragraph. Leaving this space is called indenting.

USING COMMAS

The comma is the most commonly used punctuation mark, so it is very important to understand how to use it properly.

1 **Commas are used to enable readers to see clearly the separate items in a list.**
  e.g. In his bag he had an exercise book, his running kit, a pencil, pen, ruler and a can of coke. (Note that usually a comma is not used before the final item in the list when the word 'and' is used between the last two items.)

2 **Commas are used to separate words such as 'however' or phrases such as 'of course' from the rest of the sentence.**
  e.g. However, there were many other reasons, of course, which led to the outbreak of this particular war.

3 **Commas are used to mark off short phrases that are used either at the beginning or in the middle of a sentence.**
  e.g. In 1935, Mauna Loa, the world's largest active volcano, erupted.

4 **Commas are used in longer sentences to mark off clauses.**
  e.g. If a volcano erupts under the sea, a new island may form. When the Prime Minister lost the vote of confidence, he resigned.

5 **When a sentence consists of two parts joined by a conjunction, a comma is used before the conjunction.**
  e.g. Many people smoke cigarettes, even though they know it is bad for their health.
  Fires have always been common on the savannah, so the trees have thick barks.

USING APOSTROPHES

There are two main uses of the apostrophe.

Apostrophes of omission

Sometimes, especially when we speak, we join two words together to form one word. When this happens, a letter or two letters are missed out. We show this by putting an apostrophe where the letter(s) have been missed out.

For example, **do not** becomes **don't** e.g. I don't agree; **I am** becomes **I'm** e.g. I'm not sure; and **he is** becomes **he's** e.g. he's mad.

Apostrophes of possession

An apostrophe is also used to show that something belongs to someone or something. The basic rule is that if the word that has the possession is singular you add **'s** e.g. Louisa's diary, and that if the word that has the possession is plural and ends in **s** you only add an apostrophe e.g. the students' essays or the elephants' enclosure.

| •• | IN PAIRS | •• |

Read about how commas are used. Study Examples A and B and talk about how and why the commas have been put where they are in each sentence.

Example A

In July 1914, when Archduke Ferdinand, the heir to the Austro-Hungarian throne, was assassinated, it set off a chain of events which began the First World War.

Example B

Krakatoa, a volcano on an island in Indonesia, exploded in 1883, shooting gases and lava over 16 kilometres into the air, sending up clouds of ash, so that there was darkness for two and a half days.

| •• | IN PAIRS | •• |

Study the explanations of how to use apostrophes. Then, make a list of as many examples of apostrophes of omission that you can think of. Talk about how confident you are about using apostrophes correctly.

IMPROVING YOUR SPELLING

Spelling is important for a number of reasons. If you make lots of spelling mistakes, it can distract whoever is reading your work and make it hard for them to understand what you mean. Consequently, you will lose marks in tests and examinations if you spell words wrongly. People may even jump to the wrong conclusions about the quality of your writing or how clever you are, if your work is full of spelling errors.

In order to become a good speller, you must take responsibility for improving your spelling.

- Don't rely on asking other people to tell you how to spell words you don't know.
- Use a dictionary. Look up words for yourself and think about why they are spelt as they are.
- Take care to check your spelling in all your written work, not just your English work.
- Adopt a systematic approach to learning your spellings.

How to learn your spellings

When you meet a new word and have difficulty spelling it, or when someone has pointed out that you have made a spelling mistake in your work, use a step-by-step approach to help you to learn to spell the word correctly.

1 **LOOK** at the word carefully.

2 **SAY** the word aloud, clearly and distinctly.

3 **SPLIT** the word into parts. Many words are built up from a number of parts. Breaking a word down into parts can show you how it is built up and help you to understand why it is spelt as it is.

4 **NOTICE** any tricky parts and try to invent a way of remembering them. For example, you can learn a difficult word like *necessary* by telling yourself that it has one c and two s's. If it is a word which you have misspelt, underline the part you got wrong and focus on learning that part of the word. e.g. diff**e**rent; parli**a**ment; sep**a**rate.

5 **COVER** the word and try to *write* it out from memory.
Note: It's best not to get someone to test you on your spellings by asking you to say the word out loud letter-by-letter. Spelling is a writing skill and you need to practise writing the word rather than spelling it aloud.

6 **CHECK** whether you have spelt the word correctly. If you don't get it right first time, don't just copy it out without thinking about it. Look at it again, say it aloud, focus on the part of the word you got wrong, then cover it up and try again to write it from memory.

ON YOUR OWN

It's a good idea to keep a personal spelling list similar to the one shown in Example A. Make one for yourself and use it to improve your spelling.

● Enter any difficult new words or words you have spelt wrongly in your written work on your personal spelling list.

● Use the Look-Say-Cover-Write-Check method to test your spellings.

● Put a tick in a column when you get a word right and a cross when you get it wrong.

● If you get three crosses in a row, ask an adult to help you to find a way of remembering the word.

● Don't try to learn too many words at once. Aim to learn about five words at a time.

● Try to spend a short time each day learning your spellings.

● When you have a whole page of spellings, ask a friend or an adult to test you and to help you check whether or not you have written the words correctly.

Example A

Word	Date		
	20/8/95	21/8/95	22/8/95
Ancient			
Medieval			
Alkali			
Photosynthesis			
Character			

Patterns and Structures

You can improve your spelling by becoming aware of patterns and structures that occur in English words and of some spelling rules that apply to most words.

LETTER-STRINGS

Many words begin with two or three consonants. For example, great and growth both start with the letter-string gr, while splinter and splendid both start with the letter-string spl. Certain letter-strings appear frequently in English, while others do not occur at all. For example, several English words begin with squ but no words begin sqp or sqw. As you look at English words, try to notice which letter-strings keep occurring.

PREFIXES

Many English words consist of several parts, which together create their meaning. For example, disappear consists of two parts dis + appear. It is built up by adding dis in front of the word appear. When an extra part is added in front of an existing word in this way to form another word, the extra part is known as a prefix. 'Dis' meaning 'not' is a common prefix which is found in words such as disagree and disbelieve.

Some other common prefixes are:
ante = before, anti = against, ex = out of, inter = between, mis = wrong, pre = before, pro = for or forward, re = again or back, sub = under, super = above, trans = across, un = not, under = beneath, in = not
Note: in usually becomes il before l (e.g. illegal), im before m, b and p (e.g. immoral, imbalance, improbable) and ir before r (e.g. irresponsible).

Recognising common prefixes can help you with your spelling, and with working out the meaning of new words.

SUFFIXES

A lot of words are also built up by adding an extra part to the end of an existing word. For example, the past tense of many verbs is made by adding **-ed**, e.g. disappear**ed** and attempt**ed**. When an extra part is added to the end of a word to form another word, the extra part is known as a suffix. Another common suffix is -ly which is often added to an adjective to change it into an adverb. e.g. slow + ly = slowly, usual + ly = usually.

Some other common suffixes are:
-able/ible e.g. remarkable, reversible
-ous   e.g. outrageous, courageous, furious
-ful   e.g. spiteful, tearful
-less   e.g. careless, penniless
-ment   e.g. management, encouragement
 ness   e.g. tiredness, laziness

Identifying that a word contains a suffix can often help you to work out how to spell the word correctly.

IN PAIRS

Study this list of letter-strings and say whether or not you think each letter-string is one that occurs commonly in English. Then, use a dictionary to check your answers.

phl phs phr thr ths thf gn gp gh sk sm sv sd.

Rules

● *Doubling the consonant*
When you add -ing or -ed to a word that ends in a single consonant, you must usually double the final consonant:
e.g. stop stopping stopped
This rule is true for most words, but there are some exceptions:
e.g. focus, benefit, slow

● *Put 'i' before 'e' except after 'c'.*
e.g. believe, receipt, mischief
There are some exceptions:
e.g. their, seize, weird

● *Plurals of nouns ending in 'y'.*
Change the 'y' to 'i' and add 'es':
e.g. cherry/cherries, city/cities

● *If there is a vowel before the 'y' simply add an 's':*
e.g. boy/boys, tray/trays

● *Plurals of nouns ending in 'f' change the 'f' to a 'v' and add 'es':*
e.g. thief/thieves, loaf/loaves
There are exceptions:
e.g. roof /roofs, chief/chiefs

6 Making the most of IT

HANDLING INFORMATION

It is important to learn how to use information technology, because it can help you to find, manipulate and present information.

Using databases

If you want to find a particular piece of information, such as the size of a country's population or the number of Liberal MPs that were elected in 1906, you can often find it by looking it up on a database. A database is a computerised collection of information which is stored on **records**. A collection of records is called a **datafile**. A database may contain more than one datafile, if different types of information are included in it.

All kinds of information can be stored on databases, from simple details such as the names, ages and addresses of a group of people, to detailed information about a country's industrial output. A database can store huge amounts of information, and once you know how to retrieve it, you can find the information you want very quickly.

There are databases available on a wide range of topics, and they can help you with your studies and investigations in many different subjects.

USING DATABASES TO FIND INFORMATION

In History Databases can be used to check historical facts. For example, a database on the Romans can be used to check the year in which Julius Caesar visited Britain or the date when Hadrian's Wall was built.

The information contained in databases can also help you to analyse and interpret historical evidence. For example, there are database programs available which contain the records of the censuses that were taken in certain parts of the country in the nineteenth century. This information can be used to draw conclusions about such things as the age distribution of the population, the size of families and the patterns of employment at that time.

In Science Databases can be used in science to research information and to check information collected during observations. For example, if you are doing an investigation into the creatures that live in a certain environment, you can use a database to give you information about the creatures usually found in such an environment

Then, when you have carried out your own observations, you can go back to the database and use it to help you identify and classify any of the creatures you have observed living there.

There are several database programs which contain detailed information about different countries around the world. One example is *The Times Electronic World Map and Database*. It not only offers basic information about each country's size, its population and major cities, but contains a series of datafiles that provide details on a wide range of other aspects such as government, health, education, agriculture and industry.

In Geography

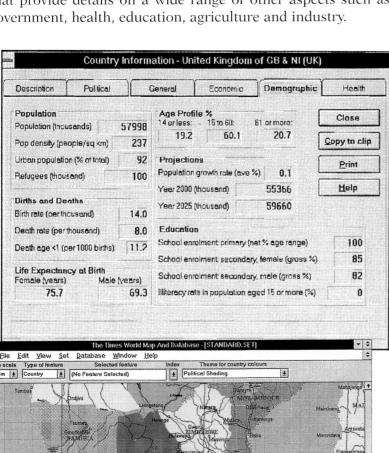

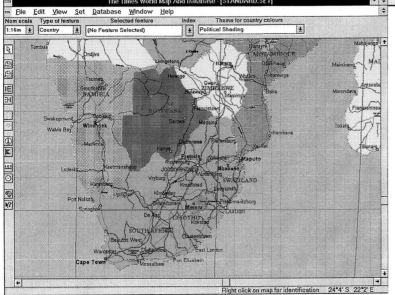

Work together to produce your own database of information about the world's volcanoes. Discuss how you are going to organise your database. Make a list of volcanoes and of the details about each volcano which you think it would be useful to include. Then, carry out the necessary research to find out the information you require, and create your database.

USING DATABASES TO RECORD INFORMATION

Many database programs are designed to enable you not only to locate information, but also to edit and update it and to add new information. You can also create your own database. For example, databases can be used to record information collected during investigations or fieldwork. You could set up a database about the local climate and enter weather data, such as measurements of temperature and rainfall.

Create a datafile for inclusion in a database about your local area, providing information on one of the following: leisure facilities, places of worship, historical sites and buildings, medical services.

Using a spreadsheet

A spreadsheet is a type of computer program which can store and manipulate large amounts of data. A spreadsheet program is used to do mathematical calculations based on the data it stores. Many spreadsheet programs also have facilities to produce graphs from the data.

Therefore, spreadsheets can help you to do calculations and to produce statistical evidence as part of investigations and experiments, and to present that information in the form of charts or graphs.

USING SPREADSHEETS

Alice was studying the density of the population in several South American countries. She found out the area of these countries and the size of their populations, then used a spreadsheet program to calculate the population density of each country.

IN PAIRS

Discuss how you could use a spreadsheet program as part of an investigation into a comparison between the climate in your area and the climate of a holiday resort in southern Italy.

Write down your ideas, then share them in a class discussion.

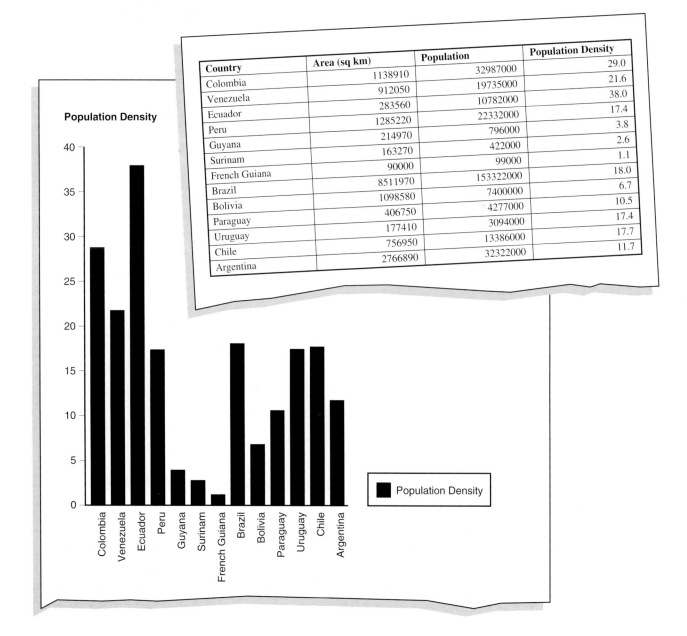

Country	Area (sq km)	Population	Population Density
Colombia	1138910	32987000	29.0
Venezuela	912050	19735000	21.6
Ecuador	283560	10782000	38.0
Peru	1285220	22332000	17.4
Guyana	214970	796000	3.8
Surinam	163270	422000	2.6
French Guiana	90000	99000	1.1
Brazil	8511970	153322000	18.0
Bolivia	1098580	7400000	6.7
Paraguay	406750	4277000	10.5
Uruguay	177410	3094000	17.4
Chile	756950	13386000	17.7
Argentina	2766890	32322000	11.7

Using a word processor

A word processing program is a computer program which enables you to enter text, manipulate it on a screen, and to print it out. Learning how to use a word processor is important, because it can help you to develop your drafting skills and improve the presentation of your work.

WHAT YOU CAN DO WITH A WORD PROCESSOR

- enter handwritten text or create new text
- make alterations to the text on the screen by inserting or deleting words
- rearrange the order of words, sentences or paragraphs
- use the program to check for spelling and typing errors, and make the corrections quickly
- save the text onto a disk and then go back to it later to revise it
- change the appearance and size of the document you are creating e.g. by altering the typeface
- print out a copy at any point, so that you can show it to someone else or work on it by hand.

DRAFTING USING A WORD PROCESSOR

You can use a word processor to draft all kinds of pieces of writing - letters, reports, essays or stories. The main advantage of using a word processor for drafting is that it can save you time. You can make changes to your drafts more quickly and easily than if you are writing by hand and have to copy out the whole piece of work to incorporate any changes.

Exactly how you draft your work on a word processor will depend on the type of writing you are doing and the method that works best for you. However, it is often useful to take a step-by-step approach:

○ ON YOUR OWN ○

Using a word processor, draft a letter to your local newspaper giving your views on an issue about the local environment which concerns you.

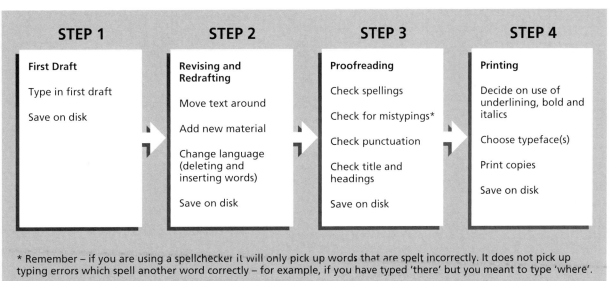

STEP 1	STEP 2	STEP 3	STEP 4
First Draft Type in first draft Save on disk	**Revising and Redrafting** Move text around Add new material Change language (deleting and inserting words) Save on disk	**Proofreading** Check spellings Check for mistypings* Check punctuation Check title and headings Save on disk	**Printing** Decide on use of underlining, bold and italics Choose typeface(s) Print copies Save on disk

* Remember – if you are using a spellchecker it will only pick up words that are spelt incorrectly. It does not pick up typing errors which spell another word correctly – for example, if you have typed 'there' but you meant to type 'where'.

DESIGNING DOCUMENTS

You can do a great deal of design work on a document using a word processor. However, for detailed design work you may find a desktop publishing (DTP) program more suitable, because it offers you a wider range of design facilities.

DTP enables you to can produce all kinds of documents, such as posters, advertisements, leaflets, information sheets and newspaper articles. You can design page lay-outs, create graphics, and use a range of different typefaces and type sizes. Developing your desktop publishing skills is important, because they will help you to learn not only how to design documents, so that you can present ideas and information effectively, but also how to analyse and criticise the documents that you read.

Developing a DTP project

Whatever kind of document you are preparing, there are certain things you need to do. Desktop publishing involves far more than simply producing a document that looks decorative and neat. Use the following checklist to help you to carry out your DTP projects successfully.

Planning

● Decide on the information you want to get across. Think about who is going to read the document. Study examples of documents similar to the one you are producing.

● Do some preliminary sketches. Make a mock-up using the actual size of paper you plan to use. If it's a leaflet, think about how you are going to fold it.

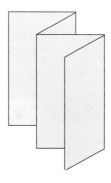 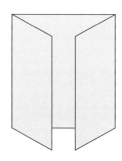

Two ways of folding a leaflet

● Think about the technology that is available. Will it do the job you need?

Producing the text and graphics

● Use an appropriate tone of voice for the document you are producing e.g. formal for a newspaper editorial, lively and enthusiastic for a holiday brochure.

● Think about how best to divide up the text and where to put headings.

● Decide where to use lists, tables, notes or diagrams rather than continuous text.

Organising the pages

- Decide what kind of layout you are going to use. You need to define the number of columns you require on a page and the distance between them. You can set this up on the screen which will show your design by displaying lines splitting the page into the columns you are going to use. This is called a grid. One of the most important considerations when deciding on the layout of your page is that the line length is short enough to be read easily. If you have an A4 page and you use the whole width, it is difficult to read and looks cluttered. It is better to have a large margin which you leave empty or use for headings, or to put the text in two or more columns like a newspaper. On a document that has small chunks of text, such as in a magazine or catalogue, it is often a good idea to use several columns across the page as this allows pictures to be inserted in a variety of ways.

- If it's a leaflet or a booklet, think about how readers are going to find what is in it. Do you need page numbers, a title page, a contents page or an index?

- Decide if there needs to be a front page or cover.

Choosing the type

- Think about the typefaces that are available. When you choose a typeface think about how easy it is to read, as well as how it looks. There are two kinds of typeface: serif, which is quite ornate, and sans serif, which is quite plain.

- Experiment with type size, spaces between the lines, and line lengths.

Checking the document

- Check for spelling errors and mistypings.

- Make sure that any pictures and diagrams are in the right place and have the correct captions.

- Check that headings are in the right place and that they are clear. It is best to leave a space between any headings and the body of text to make them stand out.

- Check that your punctuation is correct and that you have used paragraphs properly. Paragraphs should be displayed with either the first line of each paragraph indented or with a space between each paragraph.

- Check that you have used capitals correctly for proper names and that I is always a capital.

- Make sure that dates are presented correctly i.e.17(space) May (space) 1996.

- Make sure that you have put spaces after punctuation marks.

- Check that you have been consistent in your use of any underlining, bold or italic type.

Note: When you have proofread the document yourself, ask someone else to proofread it again before printing it.

◦◦◦   IN GROUPS   ◦◦◦

Practise your desktop publishing skills by designing and producing one of the following:

- a four-page insert for a teen-age magazine on a topical subject of your choice

- a publicity leaflet for a club or society (e.g. a youth club, a drama group)

- a leaflet for a pressure group urging people to support you in a campaign on an issue that concerns you.

7 Developing your oral skills

WORKING IN GROUPS

Speaking and listening in groups is a very important way of learning. It gives you a chance to try out your ideas, to listen to other people's ideas, and to work out what you really think. Therefore, you need to develop the skills that will enable you to take part in effective group work, so that you can benefit fully from the opportunities which group work offers.

SETTING UP THE GROUP

Often, your teacher will help you to set up the group by giving members of the group particular roles such as chairperson, secretary/note-taker and reporter. These roles are vital. If your teacher doesn't appoint people, then the first thing you need to do is to agree who is going to perform these roles.

The role of the chairperson

The chairperson is responsible for controlling the discussion and making sure that everyone gets a chance to join in.

The chairperson should:

1 Read out the question/instructions and get the discussion started.

2 Make sure that everyone gets a chance to speak and that one or two people do not dominate the discussion.

3 Make sure that other members of the group do not interrupt when someone else is speaking.

4 Keep the discussion focused on the task.

5 Move the discussion forward if the group gets stuck or seems to be going round and round in circles.

6 Round off the discussion and bring it to an end.

A good chairperson keeps the group in order by being calm, tactful and assertive rather than too forceful and aggressive.

The role of the secretary/note-taker

The secretary is responsible for writing down the group's views and decisions.

The secretary should:

1 Pick out and record the key points.(It is not necessary to write down everything that is said.)

2 Make a note of the different views within the group if people have not agreed on certain issues.

3 Check with the group, at the end of the discussion, that what is written down accurately sums up the group's views and decisions.

It is vital that the secretary does not allow their own opinion to influence what they write down.

The role of the reporter

The reporter is responsible for reporting the group's views to the rest of the class. In some cases, the reporter will also be the secretary. If the reporter is not the secretary, then they need to look at the secretary's notes before making their report.

The reporter should:

1 Report the discussion to the rest of the class.

2 State the reasons for the group's views and decisions.

Like the secretary, the reporter must not allow their own opinions to influence what they say, even if they disagree with what the majority of the group has said or decided.

ON YOUR OWN

Read the section about 'setting up the group'. Do you agree that the role of the chairperson is vital? Think about groups you have worked in. Which ones have worked most successfully? Which have worked least successfully?

IN PAIRS

Write a few sentences about your experiences of working in groups, and discuss what you have written.

IN GROUPS

In a group of six, choose one of the discussion topics from the list, and organise and hold a discussion. Remember to appoint three members of the group to take the roles of **a)** chairperson **b)** secretary/ reporter **c)** observer. The role of the observer is to use the group observation sheet to identify the types of comments individuals make during the discussion and to record the number of times they make each type of comment.

At the end of the discussion, get the observer to show you what they recorded on the copy of the observation sheet. Discuss what you can learn from it about the part each member of the group played in the discussion. Talk about whose contributions appear to have been most useful and why.

TAKING PART IN GROUP WORK

When you take part in a group discussion:

- **Get involved.** Don't just sit back and let others do all the talking. It's hard to know what you think until you've put your ideas into words, so join in and see what other people think of your ideas.

- **Listen carefully.** Concentrate when other people are talking, even if you think you disagree totally with what they are saying. Be prepared to be persuaded by good ideas from other people and, if appropriate, to change your opinion.

- **Give your reasons.** Always try to back up your views by giving reasons and support your statements by quoting examples.

- **Wait your turn.** Don't interrupt when someone else is putting their point of view. Wait until they have finished, and then have your say.

- **Stick to the point.** Don't start talking about something other than the subject you are meant to be discussing, or making clever comments just to get a laugh.

- **Help to keep things moving.** If the group gets stuck, see if you can suggest a way of getting the discussion going again. Perhaps you can suggest another way of tackling the problem or introduce a new idea. Alternatively, review what has been said, and see if you can re-introduce one of the points and develop it further in some way.

OBSERVING GROUPS IN ACTION

A useful way of learning about the way you perform in a group is to get someone to act as an observer and to fill in an observation sheet (such as the one on the next page) showing how often you make various types of comments during a particular discussion. Thinking about the types of comments you make can tell you how much you have been involved in a discussion and help you to think about how you might improve your contributions to group discussions in the future.

Topics for discussion

- All types of hunting should be banned.
- There should be stricter controls on horror videos and showing violence in programmes on TV.
- Parents should not be allowed to smack their children.
- Smoking should be banned in all public places.
- Children should be able to leave school at 14 if they want to do so.

GROUP WORK OBSERVATION SHEET

Each time a person speaks, decide what type of comment they make and put a tick in the appropriate column(s).
Sometimes, you may want to put a tick in more than one column.

Name and role (eg chairperson, reporter)	Introduced new ideas or opinions	Developed ideas or opinions	Listened and responded	Blocked the discussion	Interrupted the discussion	Summarised ideas and opinions	Focussed the discussion
	Introduced a new idea or opinion, suggested a new way of tackling the problem	Developed a point or by giving reasons or examples	Showed they had been listening attentively by commenting on a point made by someone else	Stopped the development of the discussion by making a frivolous or irrelevant comment	Interrupted while someone else was talking, instead of waiting for their turn	Summed up other's views clearly and accurately	Reminded group of purpose of discussion, because they were wandering off the point

This page may be photocopied

Studywise 1 © HarperCollinsPublishers 1996

MAKING A SPEECH

At certain times you will be expected to show your knowledge and understanding of a subject by talking about it – for example, by acting as the reporter for your group and explaining what you found out during an investigation. You may be asked to prepare a talk on a subject that interests you, to develop an argument expressing a particular point of view or to take part in a debate. It is important, therefore, to develop the skills you need to speak to an audience. We will focus on the skills of preparing, writing and delivering a speech.

PREPARING YOUR SPEECH

However well you think you know your subject, start by researching it thoroughly. Use your information-finding skills to *check your facts* and make sure you *keep accurate notes*. This will stop you from getting caught out in an argument because you got your facts wrong.

In addition to checking the facts, *look out for arguments* which you can use to support your point of view. Note down the *reasons* why people hold your opinion and try to find *examples* you can use as *evidence* to back up your statements. Look out, too, for the arguments people will try to use against your point of view, and note down anything you can use to counter these arguments.

Mr Speaker, my honourable friends, hear me, and be glad you can; watch me and be glad it's not from behind bars; walk to me and be glad of your freedom. Now think of the animals, the creatures in our zoos, shut in day and night, in prison, guilty of nothing but living. Oh yes, I hear you say, what about all the animals the zoos have saved from becoming extinct? What about all the species that zoos have *not* helped - for example, the marsupial wolf, cape lion or crested shellduck? Zoos are saving 20 species in a hundred years, but we are losing one every day!

You may say that zoos are educational for our children. Are they? Really? Children see a tiger pacing up and down in its cage. Is that a tiger's real nature? Is your child seeing a tiger in its natural habitat? Are zoos really educating your child? Over 60% of polar bears in our zoos are mentally ill. What are we doing about it? NOTHING! What are we doing about the deprived and mentally ill children discovered in Roumanian orphanages? Helping! What is the difference – we are all living creatures. Over half of all zoo owners have not researched their animals. They keep them in dirty cages, and only guess at the correct food. Monkeys over-groom and have bald patches. Elephants bang their heads against their concrete prison walls. Birds that are used to flying miles in wide open spaces suffer the frustration of not being able to fly more than a few metres. These are minor examples compared to some cases. You look between the bars but do you see what's there? Can you see the agony and boredom? These creatures are living, do you hear me, *living!* They are not just toys for our enjoyment.

Would you like to sit in a room for the rest of your life? NO! You would *die* of boredom, commit suicide or go insane. This is what is happening to animals in our zoos. They die before their time, wasting away because of our neglect! Is this fair I ask you? NO! These animals have a right to freedom. Are you to deprive them of their lives? Do you know the answers to these questions? I do. The answer is YES! We are *murdering* innocent creatures for our selfish greed and enjoyment. The animals' freedom and enjoyment of life have been taken away…stolen. Animals have feelings too — they are not rag dolls you can throw out when you have had enough of them. So take a second look at the tiger pacing his figure of eight, the kookaburra staring through the netting to the open sky, and the monkey swinging end-lessly on his rope. Look through the boredom: see the pain.

Kyla Hindshaw

WRITING YOUR SPEECH

There are a number of techniques you can use when writing a speech in order to make it more effective. The advice below is taken from a helpsheet which a teacher gave to a class who were going to debate the case for and against zoos.

- **Grab their attention.** Make sure you start with a statement or question that will capture the audience's attention.
  e.g. *Newspaper stories about animals in prison are grossly exaggerated. They paint a very false picture of what zoos are really like.*

- **Use facts and statistics.** Support your statements with statistics and specific examples. This adds weight to your arguments.
  e.g. *London Zoo alone costs the taxpayer 2 million pounds a year.*
  Zoos have saved many species from extinction, including the African black rhino, the snow leopard and the African elephant.

- **Include lists of three.** Statements which list things in threes are more likely to hold the audience's attention and remain in their minds.
  e.g. *Zoos play a vital role in conservation, scientific research and education.*
  Animals imprisoned in zoos become increasingly bored, insecure and confused.

- **Use alliteration.** A statement that includes a number of words starting with the same letter is likely to be more memorable.
  e.g. *Zoos provide animals with a sense of safety and security.*

- **Refer to personal experiences.** This suggests you really know what you are talking about.
  e.g. *'When I visited Paignton Zoo recently, I noticed...'*

- **Use repetition.** This helps to emphasise the point you are making.
  e.g. *60% of polar bears in captivity suffer mental distress. Yes, 60%.*
  I bet all of you have been to a zoo and I bet you enjoyed it.

- **Include questions.** These can have a dramatic effect, particularly if they are questions that do not require an answer i.e. rhetorical questions.
  e.g. *Isn't it obvious that there is no justification for locking up animals in zoos?*

- **Involve the audience.** Addressing the audience directly can help to get them on your side.
  e.g. *How would you feel if you had your freedom taken away and you had to live your life in a cage?*

- **Use sarcasm.** This can help to undermine the arguments used against you.
  e.g. *I do not think that this can be described as either conservation or education.*
  Surely you're not trying to say that people don't enjoy visiting zoos.

- **'Set them up, then knock them down.'** This is a particularly effective way of undermining the opposition's arguments.
  e.g. *You complain that animals are kept in small cages. Well, why don't you go home and set your pets free? After all, they live in even smaller cages!*

- **End emphatically.** Make sure you end your speech on a high note.
  e.g. *Don't make a decision that you'll live to regret. Once a species dies out, it can never be replaced.*

IN PAIRS

Study the advice on writing a speech, then read Kyla's speech (on page 45), which was prepared after reading and discussing the helpsheet. Go through Kyla's speech and identify which of the techniques she uses in order to make her speech effective.

DELIVERING YOUR SPEECH

There are several things you need to think about when you are delivering a speech.

- **Eye-contact.** It's important to look at the audience in order to hold their attention. That's why people often either learn a speech off by heart or use notes to remind them of its key points. This enables you to maintain eye-contact, which you cannot do if you are reading and having to look down at your script.

- **Tone.** Vary the tone of your voice. This helps to keep the audience's attention. If you speak in the same tone all the time it can become monotonous and boring for your listeners. Speak clearly and with plenty of expression.

- **Volume.** Speak up and don't mumble. Speak loudly enough for everyone to be able to hear you, but don't shout, and take care not to drop your voice towards the end of your sentences or at the end of your speech. Deliberately raising your voice occasionally is a useful way of emphasising a point.

- **Pace.** Think about the pace of your speech. If the pace is too slow, then your audience will eventually 'switch off'. If you speak too fast, then they won't be able to follow what you are saying.

- **Body language.** Stand up straight and don't slouch. Try to look confident, however nervous you are actually feeling. You can use hand gestures to emphasise key points, but don't overdo it or it will distract the audience from what you are saying.

- **Pauses.** Skilled public speakers use pauses as an effective way of stressing key points and making their delivery more dramatic. Think about using a pause after a dramatic piece of information or a rhetorical question. Again, beware of overdoing it or you might affect the pace of your speech.

ON YOUR OWN

Research and write a speech in which you present your views on an animal rights issue, such as circuses or vivisection, or on a subject which you feel strongly about, such as euthanasia or vegetarianism.

IN CLASS

Deliver your speech and get your audience to give you marks out of ten for your delivery, using the checklist of delivery techniques (on the left). Discuss with them which techniques you used effectively, and which you could improve.

ON YOUR OWN

Write a short statement commenting on how effective you think your speech was and saying what you have learned from the activity about planning, writing and delivering speeches.

8 Preparing for tests

Keep your files in order

The more organised you are, the easier it is for you to revise for tests. Many students find it hard to get started, and waste a lot of valuable time because they cannot find the notes they need. Developing a proper filing system can save you a lot of time and keep you from getting stressed.

Developing your revision skills

When you revise, it is important to use strategies that will help you to remember the facts you need to know. Don't just spend all your time reading and re-reading your notes in the hope that somehow you'll take everything in. You need to make a conscious effort to learn what you are reading, and that means working on your notes and using strategies that will help you to focus on a topic, to pick out the key facts and fix them in your mind.

A STEP-BY-STEP REVISION STRATEGY

> Use this step-by-step strategy to develop an active approach to your revision.

PRACTISE YOUR REVISION SKILLS

IN PAIRS

Study the two examples of revision cards. Both Janice and Leon were revising from notes and written answers they had done as part of their study of the rainforests in South America. Notice how Janice has chosen to use diagram notes on her card, while Leon has written numbered block notes. Discuss which set of notes you would find easier to learn.

Rain Forest Destruction
(50% lost in 50 years - 10% in 1980s)
Causes

Logging (Timber for furniture etc)   Industrial development   Mines Roads Dams   'Slash and burn' (Subsistence Farming)   Ranching (Beef cattle for burgers in U.S.)

Tribal life destroyed   Wildlife extinct   Effects   Plants (Loss of medicines)
Increased CO_2 global warming   Soil erosion and land degradation

Leon
Destruction of tropical rainforest (10% in '80s)
Causes: 1 Logging (5 million hectares per year)
2 Mining (copper, bauxite, iron ore) Roads e.g. Trans-Amazon highway Dams (for hydroelectricity)
3 Subsistence farming (slash and burn)
4 Ranching (beef)

Effects: 1 Tribal life and culture destroyed
2 Global warming (increased CO_2)
3 Loss of plant species and possible medicines
4 Extinction of wildlife
5 Land degradation due to soil erosion

Choose a topic which you have both been studying and need to learn for a test later in the term. On your own, practise your revision skills by making a revision card and learning what you need to know. Then, compare your revision cards, and test each other on what you have learned.

STEP 1

Preparation

Before you begin, make sure you have everything you need. Since you are going to be working on your notes, you will need a biro, a pencil and ruler or a highlighter pen, and some pieces of scrap paper or index cards.

STEP 2

Studying your notes

Choose one of the topics that you have to revise, and concentrate on that section of your notes. Read carefully through your notes, pick out the key facts and either underline or highlight them.

STEP 3

Make a revision card

Go through your notes again and make a set of revision notes, either on a piece of scrap paper or a card, by listing the key facts you have got to learn.

STEP 4

Learning

Study the revision card and try to learn the key facts. If there is a word you have difficulty remembering how to spell, use the look-say-cover-write-check method (see page 34) to try to learn it.

STEP 5

Testing

Either cover up the revision card and try to write out the key facts from memory, or give the card to a friend or relative and ask them to test you.

STEP 6

Checking

If you are working on your own, check to see if you got all the facts right and whether you missed any out. Use your pencil or highlighter pen to mark any important points which you did not remember and, if necessary, repeat steps 4, 5 and 6 until you are sure that you have learned what you need to know.

FINDING OUT ABOUT TESTS

To prepare yourself for tests in any of your subjects, you need to find out:

● the topics you will be tested on;

● the skills you need to learn;

● the type of questions you will be asked;

● the structure of the test e.g. How many papers are there? How long is each paper? Is there a practical test?

You can find out what you need to know by asking your teacher in order to check which topics you need to revise.

You can find out about the structure of the test and the type of questions you will be expected to answer by looking at examples of past papers.

IN PAIRS

Study the instructions on the front of the 1995 Key Stage 3 Science paper 1 for Tier 5-7. Discuss what you learn from these instructions about the structure of the test e.g. about the time allowed, the equipment you will need, the level of the questions, which questions you have to answer and where you have to write your answers.

Key Stage 3   1995

SCIENCE

Tier 5-7

Paper 1

Please read this page, but do not open the booklet until your teacher tells you to start. Write your name and school in the spaces below. If you have been given a pupil number, write that also. In Wales, write your date of birth instead of a pupil number.

First Name_____ Last Name_____

School _____

Pupil Number [ ][ ][ ][ ][ ][ ]   Total Marks [ ]

Remember

· The test is 1 hour long.

· You will need a pen, a pencil, a rubber, a ruler and a calculator.

· The first part of this paper has questions on levels 5 and 6. The second part has questions on level 7.

· Try to answer all of the questions. If you find a question too hard, go on to the next question.

· Write all your answers in the booklet. Do not use any rough paper.

· Check your work carefully.

· Ask your teacher if you are not sure what to do.

TACKLING TESTS

IN THE WEEKS BEFORE THE TEST

Plan a revision programme. Make a list of the topics you need to revise, and draw up a revision timetable. Make sure you include some time for relaxing. Don't start staying up late to work. If you get too tired, you won't be able to revise properly.

THE NIGHT BEFORE THE TEST

Do not do too much last-minute revising. If you do, you are likely to tire yourself out mentally. Read through a few of the most important revision cards. Then, sort out the clothes you are going to wear the next day and set out the equipment you need for the test, so you won't be rushed in the morning. Find something relaxing to do before you go to bed, such as reading or watching TV. Make sure you don't go to bed too late, but do not start worrying if you don't fall asleep immediately.

THE DAY OF THE TEST

Don't try to do any revision. Try to get to the room where the test is being held a few minutes early – you don't want to start the test feeling flustered because you arrived late. Try not to get drawn into conversations with your friends about what revision they've done and what questions you are likely to be asked.

IN THE TEST

● Check that you have been given the right paper.

● Read the instructions on the front of the paper to make sure you understand what you have to do.

● When you are tackling a question, reread the question carefully to understand exactly what it is asking.

● Note any advice you are given about how much time to spend on each section.

● If there is a clock in the room, set your watch to agree with it. Note the exact time when the test starts, so that you will be able to check during the test how much time you have left.

● If you have a choice of questions, read all the questions and put ticks beside the ones you think you can do.

● Note how many marks it carries. Don't waste time giving too detailed an answer to a questions which only carries one or two marks.

● Leave yourself enough time at the end to read through your answers to check for careless mistakes and spelling errors.

● If you think you are running out of time, try to write short answers in note-form or to list the main points. This should help you to pick up more marks than if you go on writing detailed answers and fail to finish the paper.

●●   IN PAIRS   ●●

Study the advice that is given on this page about how to tackle tests. Each choose five pieces of advice that you find useful and together discuss the reasons for your choice. Then, look at all of the advice, divide a piece of paper into two columns, one labelled Do's and one labelled Don'ts, and produce a chart, 'How to tackle tests – Some Do's and Don'ts.'

A Testing Problem

Dear Maxine,

My problem is that I never seem to do very well in tests. I do lots of revising and I always stay up late the night before, doing last-minute revision. But I get flustered during the test and make silly mistakes, like answering all four questions when you're only supposed to do one. I worry about whether I've got the right answers and whether my spellings are correct. I just can't seem to concentrate properly and I often run out of time. Then, when the results come out, I get very depressed. What can I do?

Nicoletta

ON YOUR OWN

Study Nicoletta's letter to a teenage magazine's problem page. Draft the reply that you would write, if you were Maxine. Then, hold a class discussion in which you read out your replies and decide which of your answers gives Nicoletta the best advice.

9 Recording Your Progress

ASSESSING YOUR SKILLS

At least once a year, it is important to look back and to think about what progress you have made during the year. Here is a list of skills which you are learning as a result of the work you do in your different lessons. Use the questions under each skill to help you to decide what progress you have made in each skill over the past year.

Communication Skills

● **Speaking and listening**
1 Are you better at preparing talks and speeches and at giving oral reports?
2 Are you more confident about expressing your point of view?
3 Do you take more part in group discussions?
4 Have your listening skills improved?

● **Writing**
1 Are you better at writing reports and conveying information?
2 Have you improved your essay-writing skills? Are you better at presenting an argument and using evidence to support your ideas?
3 Are you better at planning and drafting your work?
4 Has the accuracy of your spelling and punctuation improved?

● **Reading**
1 Has your reading ability developed this year? Are you now able to read and understand more complex information?
2 Have you improved your reading strategies, e.g. your ability to skim and scan?
3 Have you improved your ability to analyse and interpret texts?

Number Skills

1 Has your ability to handle numerical information improved?
2 Has your ability to collect and present numerical information in different ways improved?

Study Skills

1 Are you better at planning your study schedule and organising your home work?
2 Have your research skills developed? Are you better at finding information from different sources?
3 Has your ability to take good notes and to record information improved?
4 Are you better at organising your revision and at preparing for tests?

Using the lists of questions think about each skill in turn, and write a short comment saying how much you think you have improved that skill over the past year – a lot, quite a lot, only a little. Support your statement by referring to things that you have done during the year.

For example, here is part of Jennifer's comment on her IT skills:

> I think my IT skills have improved a lot this year. I learned how to use a database in history. I also developed some desktop publishing skills during the newspaper project, like how to lay out a page in different ways.

Show the comments to a friend. Talk about your strengths and weaknesses, and each decide on two skills at which you are rather weak and which you need to concentrate on developing.

Problem Solving Skills
1   Are you better at organising and developing your projects and assignments?
2   Has your ability to plan investigations and enquiries improved?
3   Has your ability to collect data in different ways and to make observations improved?
4   Are you better at analysing results, forming opinions and drawing conclusions?
5   Are you better at thinking things through and at making suggestions and offering solutions to problems?

Personal and Social Skills
1   Are you better at taking responsibility for organising your time?
2   Has your knowledge of your own strengths and weaknesses increased?
3   Are you more self-confident than you were a year ago?
4   Have you worked well in groupwork during the year, helping to solve problems that have arisen? Has your ability to be a good team member developed?
5   Are you better at making decisions?
6   Are you better at listening to and understanding other people and seeing things from their point of view?

Information Technology Skills
1   Are you better at finding and manipulating data on computers?
2   Have your word-processing skills improved?
3   Are you better at using a computer for drafting and editing a piece of writing?
4   Have you learned more about how to use computers to produce documents?
5   Have your desktop publishing skills improved?

RECORDING YOUR ACHIEVEMENTS

Use this step-by-step approach to review what you have achieved in the past year and to record your achievements.

Step 1 **A** Make a list of each of the subjects you are studying. Think about each subject in turn and write a comment saying how you think you have done in that subject during the year. Give a reason for what you think. If you think your work in history is better, say why you think it is better. For example, 'I think I've done better in history because I've learned how to look for biased views when I read historical documents.' If you are finding a subject difficult, try to explain why you are finding it difficult.

B If you have not already done so, assess your progress in developing your skills (see pages 52-53).

C Make a list of all the activities you have been involved in during the year – both in and out of school. Include any clubs and societies to which you belong, any school activities which you have taken part in – plays, concerts, assemblies, sports, trips, tutor-group activities – and any outside activities, personal hobbies and interests. Write down what you think have been your most significant achievements in these activities during the past year.

Step 2 **A** Arrange a meeting with your tutor in order to discuss your view of your progress and achievements. Show your tutor what you have written about your subjects and your activities, and tell them what you identified as your strengths and weaknesses when you assessed your skills (pages 52-53).

B During the meeting, listen carefully to what your tutor has to say. Write down anything which they point out you have missed out and note down what they say if they disagree with your assessment, either because they think you are being too harsh on yourself or because they feel you have overestimated what you have achieved.

Step 3 **A** Draft a statement about your achievements over the past year. Include comments on your subjects, your skills and your activities, both in and out of school.

B Show your statement to your tutor and produce a final copy, which both you and your tutor agree is a correct record of your achievements.

C File your statement in your record of achievements folder.

SETTING TARGETS

Reviewing your progress and recording your achievements is useful not only because it can help you to recognise what has gone well, but also because it can help you to identify those areas that you need to concentrate on improving. When you have identified a skill or a subject that you need to improve, you can set yourself a target and draw up an action plan.

MAKING AN ACTION PLAN

It is usually much easier to set yourself a target than to decide how you are going to achieve it. It is important, therefore, to have a clear plan. You can divide your target into separate steps and set dates to be the deadlines when you will review the progress of your plan.

Make sure that the target you set is a realistic one. For example, you could set yourself a short-term goal of making some improvement within a few weeks, and a long-term goal of making a significant improvement over the whole year.

Try to get someone to support you in your attempts to achieve your goal. There are a number of people who might be able to give you support – for example, your subject teacher, your tutor or one of your parents. It is often better to have an adult to support you, but if none is available, then you could ask a friend to help.

Here is the action plan drawn up by Justin who wants to do better in Geography:

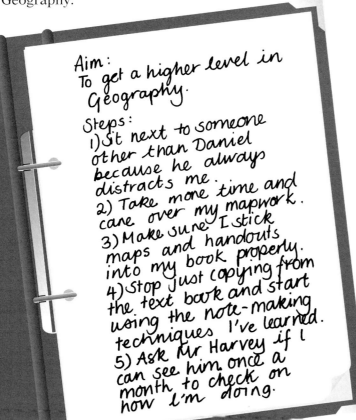

Aim:
To get a higher level in Geography.

Steps:
1) Sit next to someone other than Daniel because he always distracts me.
2) Take more time and care over my mapwork.
3) Make sure I stick maps and handouts into my book properly.
4) Stop just copying from the text book and start using the note-making techniques I've learned.
5) Ask Mr Harvey if I can see him once a month to check on how I'm doing.

ON YOUR OWN

Look back at the comments you wrote about your subjects and your skills. Decide which skills and subjects you'd most like to improve during the next year. For each one, think about what you would have to do and the things you might have to change in order to improve in that subject or skill. Then, decide on two or three targets and draw up an action plan for each one. When you have finished, show your action plans to a partner and discuss them.

10 Thinking about your future

WHAT ARE YOUR INTERESTS?

Which activities do you enjoy doing? Which activities do you dislike doing? Thinking about your interests and your likes and dislikes is a good way of starting to think about your future. It can help you as you begin to consider which courses you would like to study and which career you might like to follow.

Here is what Amanda wrote when she was asked to answer some questions about her interests and to think about what the answers told her about herself:

Write down three things which you like doing.

I like mending things and taking things apart to see how they work. I enjoyed having to strip my bike down and mend it after I fell off and it got damaged.
I enjoyed helping with the lights when we put on the lower school play.
I like going to the youth club and helping to organise things, like getting things ready for the disco.

Write down three things which you don't like doing.

I don't like having to write stories. I can never think what to write.
I don't like sports, particularly team games.
I don't like speaking in front of lots of people. I hated it when we had to put on an assembly.

What is your favourite subject?

Technology. I really enjoyed designing and making a toy. I made a spaceship with a motor in it.

What is your least favourite subject?

French. I can't remember the words and even if I do, I can never spell them right.

What have you learned about yourself from thinking about your interests?

I think it tells me I'm a practical sort of person, and that I'm interested in technical things.

ON YOUR OWN

Think about your interests, and write about your likes and dislikes, and your favourite and least favourite subjects, in the way that Amanda has done. Then, answer the question: What have you learned about yourself from thinking about your interests? (If you have difficulty in answering this question, show an adult what you have written and discuss it with them.)

WHAT ARE YOUR STRENGTHS AND SKILLS?

Everyone has particular strengths and skills. Skills don't just mean the study skills that you were thinking about when you were reviewing your progress (pages 52-3). There are skills involved in the way you behave towards other people and how you react in all kinds of everyday situations. When you are thinking about your future, you need to think about your personal qualities and what your particular strengths are.

Here is what Tom and Yasmin wrote when they were asked to study the list of personal qualities (right) and to think about their strengths:

> I think I showed determination when I was learning how to skate. I kept on falling over and people laughed at me, but I just got up and kept on trying until I could do it. — Tom

> I think I'm a caring person. My mum works with old people and I sometimes go along with her in the holidays. I like talking to the old people and taking them out into the garden. Yasmin

PERSONAL QUALITIES

Caring
Consideration
Courage
Determination
Empathy
Humour
Imagination
Initiative
Kindness
Leadership
Patience
Perseverance
Reliability
Responsibility
Sympathy
Tact
Teamwork
Tolerance
Trust
Unselfishness

ON YOUR OWN

● Study the list of personal qualities. (If you don't understand some of these words, look them up in a dictionary.) What are your particular strengths? Write about your own particular strengths in the way that Tom and Yasmin have, and give examples of situations in which you have shown those strengths.

● Another way of thinking about your strengths and skills is to think about how you would cope in certain situations. Study the list of situations (below) and rate how well you think you would be able to cope in each situation on a ten-point scale: 10 = Extremely well; 1 = Unable to cope. Be honest! There is no point in pretending you would be able to cope, if you know that you wouldn't. When you have finished, try to think of two more situations in which you would cope very well.

IN PAIRS

● Share your ratings with a friend and discuss what this exercise tells you about your strengths.

● Matching your skills with the skills you need for different jobs will help you to think about possible future careers. Use the careers library or a careers CD Rom or database to find out the skills that are needed for a job which interests you. Do you have the right skills or could you develop them?

HOW WOULD YOU COPE...

1 If you had to cook a two-course dinner for 4 people?

2 If you had to give first aid to a person after an accident?

3 If you had to look after a 6-month-old baby in an emergency?

4 If you had to give a speech to an audience of 50 people?

5 If you were asked to draft a petition protesting about something on behalf of your classmates?

6 If your bicycle was broken and there was no one but you to mend it?

7 If you were asked to design a logo for a new school society?

8 If a radiator started to leak while you were alone in the house?

9 If you had to learn a new language because your family suddenly moved to a foreign country?

10 If you were asked to organise a class outing?

WHAT DO YOU WANT FROM A JOB OR CAREER?

I would like to work:

in a lively atmosphere ☐

in a quiet atmosphere ☐

outdoors ☐

indoors ☐

from home ☐

in lots of different places ☐

I would prefer to wear:

a uniform ☐

smart clothes ☐

casual clothes ☐

scruffy clothes ☐

I want to work:

with others ☐

helping others ☐

organising others ☐

on my own ☐

I would like people to:

respect me ☐

envy me ☐

like me ☐

I would be prepared to work:

every hour I can ☐

from nine to five ☐

in flexible shifts ☐

I want to earn:

as much as I can ☐

a good wage ☐

more than my parents ☐

whatever the job I enjoy pays ☐

The most important thing to me is:

how much money I earn ☐

the convenience of my job ☐

that I am challenged by my job ☐

that I am helping others ☐

that I am doing something worthwhile ☐

PLACE

CLOTHES

PEOPLE

STATUS

TIME

MONEY

PRIORITIES

ON YOUR OWN

Complete this quiz. Then use the careers library or a careers CD Rom to find out about careers that interest you and see whether they fit in with what you think you want.

WHAT OPPORTUNITIES ARE THERE FOR YOU AT 16+?

The decisions you take at fourteen can affect what you are able to do at sixteen. Therefore, it is important, when you make your option choices, to consider what pathways will be open to you at sixteen.

•• IN PAIRS ••

Study the information (right). What are the main differences between the three pathways? What do you think are the main advantages and disadvantages of each of the three pathways?

Looking ahead, which pathway do you think you might follow in the future?

Bear in mind that, to some extent, your choice may depend on what is actually available in your area. Work together and collect more information about the choices open to you at 16+ by studying your school's sixth-form brochure, finding out what courses your local college runs for 16-19 year olds and contacting your local careers service. Then, share the information you have gathered in a class discussion about choices at 16+.

PATHWAYS AT 16+

Most 16-19 year olds follow pathways that involve continuing in full-time or part-time education or training. A small number leave school and go into jobs with no training or, if they are unsuccessful in their search for work, they become unemployed.

The majority of 16-19 year olds are following one of three pathways:

ACADEMIC PATHWAY

A general education course at school or college

If you have got the required GCSE or Standard Grades, you can go on to do A levels and AS levels or to study for your Highers. Most people do either three A levels, or two A levels and two AS levels, or four or five Scottish Highers. The A level and AS level courses take two years, while the Highers takes one-year.

Some people stay on at school, or go to college, to do extra GCSEs or Standard Grades, or to do retakes in order to try to improve their grades. They may need certain grades to apply for a particular job, or to be accepted on an A level course.

VOCATIONAL PATHWAY

A vocational educational course at school or college

If you want to have some training, but are unsure as to precisely what job you want to do, you can start a GNVQ or GSVQ course. GNVQ stands for General National Vocational Qualification and GSVQ for General Scottish Vocational Qualification. GNVQ and GSVQ courses enable you to learn skills that are suitable for the jobs available in each of fifteen particular vocational areas, such as Health and Social Care, Business, or Engineering, rather than offering you training for a specific job. GNVQ and GSVQ courses are offered at three levels - Foundation, Intermediate and Advanced – and are one or two-year full-time courses. The level you start at will depend on the levels you achieved in your GCSEs or Standard Grades.

Depending on the course and the level you are taking, you may be able to study for other qualifications while you are doing your GNVQ or GSVQ. For example, you may be able to take one or two GCSEs with a Foundation or Intermediate level GNVQ, or an A level, or the AS equivalent, with an Advanced GNVQ.

OCCUPATIONAL PATHWAY

A course of training for a particular job

People who leave school at sixteen to start work can often follow a training course whilst they are working, which leads to a National Vocational Qualification (NVQ) or Scottish Vocational Qualification (SVQ). There are several hundred NVQs. An NVQ develops the skills you need to be able to do a particular job. An NVQ course may last as long as two years, and you may have to attend college for some parts of the course. There are NVQs at five levels ranging from basic to professional and managerial, with levels 4 and 5 equivalent to higher education qualifications.

11 Choosing your courses

WHAT COURSES CAN I CHOOSE AT 14?

The courses you can choose will depend on how the curriculum is organised at your school. Some schools offer the same curriculum to all students, but in many schools you will have to make choices between certain subjects. Below are the answers to some of the questions you are likely to want to ask.

Q *Are there any subjects that everyone has to take?*

A Yes, the National Curriculum has made certain subjects compulsory. These are often referred to as 'core subjects'. Everyone has to study Mathematics, English, Science, Technology, a Modern Language and Religious Education. However, in your school other subjects may also be compulsory. How much choice you actually have varies from school to school.

Q *If I can choose my science course, should I take Double Science, Single Science, or all three Sciences?*

A In some schools everyone has to take Double Science. In order to go on to study an A level Science subject (Biology, Chemistry or Physics) you will need a pass (A-C) in either Double Science GCSE or in the particular Science you want to study.

Q *Are there any other subjects that I must do at GCSE if I want to do them at A level?*

A Yes, if you want to take an A level in Maths or Languages, you must study them at GCSE. You are also advised to take GCSE Music, Art and English Literature if you think you might want to study any of those subjects at A level.

Q *What are half-subjects?*

A Your school may offer certain combinations of half-subjects to allow you to go on studying a wider range of subjects, in order to keep more pathways open for you at 16+. For example, you may be able to do Geography combined with History or Religious Studies, or Technology combined with Business Studies, IT or a Language. The two half-subjects together form a GCSE course and you will get a single GCSE grade at the end of the course.

Q *Can I start a vocational course at 14?*

A That will depend on your school. Some schools have already introduced courses that enable their pupils to start working towards vocational qualifications. More and more schools are likely to do so in the future. The advantage of beginning a vocational course at this stage of your school career is that it can add variety to the type of work you do, and enable you to start developing skills that will be useful to you in a career in the future.

•• IN PAIRS ••

Study your school's Year 10 Courses Guide. Which subjects are compulsory? What choice of subjects do you have to make? Are certain subjects blocked together on the timetable, so you can only choose one subject from each block?

Discuss what you have learned from this page about which subjects you must do at GCSE if you want to do them at A level. What do you learn from Kelly's story (on page 61) about her vocational course? Are there any vocational courses offered at your school? If so, are you considering doing one of them?

Kelly's story

Kelly (15) chose a vocational course in Business Administration, together with 7 GCSEs. It will provide her with important skills which will help her follow a vocational pathway at 16+ rather than an academic pathway.

She values the skills that she has gained in data processing, typing, filing, handling of petty cash, invoicing and stock control.

'It's not like normal lessons. With this you are learning something that you are definitely going to need,' she says. 'Some of the tasks could be more challenging – things like filing can be a bit boring – but if you don't work, you don't pass.'

She has become self-motivated, undertaking as much work as possible in her own time. During work experience she has spent time in the school office and at Boots the Chemist. 'It makes you realise how important it is to be able to do things like maths,' she says. 'And it makes you work at your other subjects. I think I'll do well at my GCSEs, but I'd rather do this practical kind of work.'

(adapted from *The Independent* 29 September 1994)

Getting further information and advice

● From your form teacher

When you have studied the Year 10 Courses booklet, if you are still unsure how the options system works in your school, ask your teacher to explain it to you. Your teacher will also help you to consider your strengths and weaknesses, which you identified when you reviewed your progress, when you choose your options.

● From your subject teachers

If you want to know more about what a particular course involves, ask your subject teacher. Find out which syllabus you will be studying and ask about what it contains, what coursework you will have to do and how you will be tested in the end-of-course examination. Ask them to explain what skills you need to have in order to do well in that subject at GCSE.

● From the careers department

If you want to find out what qualifications are required for a particular job, you can use the careers section in your school library or ask the careers teacher for information.

● From your parents

Talk to your parents about the careers you are interested in and the choices you have got to make. Discuss your ideas with them and listen to any suggestions they may make. However, do not let their opinions push you towards doing something that you do not really want to do. Remember that it is *your* future that is being discussed and the final decisions must be yours.

● From the local careers service

Contact the local careers service who can help you by providing information on the careers that you might be interested in and the qualifications you need for them.

●●●   IN GROUPS   ●●●

Make a list of all the jobs that people in the group are interested in, and then find out information about them.

●●●●   IN CLASS   ●●●●

Use the information each group has discovered to create a database about different jobs.

Useful Books

Two useful books offering information and advice are:

Your GCSE decisions by Alan Vincent published by Trotman & Co

13+ Pathways to Success by Karen Gold published by CRAC (The Careers Research and Advisory Centre)

MAKING UP YOUR OWN MIND

When you are deciding which subjects to choose, it is important to consider what your motives are for choosing particular subjects and what the consequences of your choices will be. When you are selecting your subjects, you need to consider these points:

● **Careers**

Although you may have an idea about the type of career you would like to follow, it is quite likely that you will change your mind in the future. Instead of making a narrow choice of subjects, keep your options open by selecting a broad range of subjects, which could lead to a number of different careers.

● **Interests**

Once you have started a course, you probably won't be able to change it. Each of your courses will usually involve three or four periods of classwork per week, plus a considerable amount of homework and coursework. Therefore, it is very important to choose subjects which genuinely interest you.

● **Skills**

Different subjects require different skills and talents. The subjects in which you are already achieving good grades are more likely to be those in which you will achieve examination success. Think carefully before you decide to drop a subject in which you are doing well.

● **Teachers**

Do not choose a subject simply because you like the teacher who has been teaching you that subject. Similarly, don't avoid a subject because you do not like a particular teacher. The chances are that you will not be taught by the same teacher anyway. Whether you are interested in the subject, and whether or not you have the skills to do the subject are far more important than whether or not you like the teacher.

● **Friends**

Do not choose a subject because you think it will enable you to be with your friends. Choosing a subject because a friend is going to do it is not a good reason. Besides, there is no guarantee that you would be with your friend anyway. In many subjects, there will be more than one set or class, so you may not be put in the same group as your friend.

Using a careers library

All careers libraries are organised in the same way. They use a system known as the Careers Library Classification Index (CLCI) to file information on different jobs. Each type of job is given its own two- or three-letter code which you can find by looking in a booklet which contains an alphabetical list of jobs with their codes. Similar jobs are given similar codes. For example, engineering jobs are filed under codes beginning with the letter R. Within group R you can find information about jobs in aeronautical and space engineering (RAC), automobile engineering (RAE), electronic engineering (RAL) and many other types of engineering.

Whenever you are using a careers library, be sure to glance at all the jobs that are classified in any group. You may notice another job which you had not thought of but which looks very interesting.

Five *Do's* and *Don'ts* for Decisions

You will have to live with the decisions you make about GCSE/Standard Grades for the next two years. Some of the decisions may be easy, but some will be more difficult. So make sure you don't rush into them.

- **DO** give yourself several weeks.
- **DO** find out the facts you need.
- **DO** get advice from experts.
- **DO** weigh up the arguments.
- **DO** have a fall-back plan.
- **DON'T** leave it to the last minute.
- **DON'T** guess you'll get it right.
- **DON'T** be swayed by gossip.
- **DON'T** let someone else decide for you.
- **DON'T** give up if you can't get what you want.

●●●   IN GROUPS   ●●●

Discuss each of the statements from pupils explaining why they decided to choose or give up a certain subject. Decide which reasons you think are good reasons and which you think are bad reasons.

A GOOD REASON?

Here are the reasons which twelve pupils gave for choosing or giving up a particular subject:

I couldn't make up my mind which subject to take in one of the option blocks, so I talked it over with my parents and let them decide. **Alison**

I'm far more interested in it than in the other subjects, even though my grades are slightly lower. **Pat**

It was simple to choose, because I've made up my mind what I'm going to do in the future. **Liam**

I've been struggling in that subject ever since I started it, there doesn't seem much point in choosing it when I can start something else. **Lorraine**

I can't stand the teacher we've got, so I'm giving it up. **Graham**

It'll give me a good range of different subjects if I choose that one. **Justine**

My friend's chosen that subject, so I've chosen it too. **Sharon**

My teacher thinks I shouldn't drop the subject. **Nasreen**

I just chose the subjects I find easy. I don't want to waste the whole of the next two years working. **Andy**

It's not a subject that I'm particularly good at, but you need it for lots of different careers. **Javed**

It won't help towards my career, but it's something I really enjoy. **Neil**

A STEP-BY-STEP APPROACH

Use this step-by-step approach to help you to make your decisions and choose your options.

STEP 1
– Find out the facts

About the courses
Which subjects do you have to choose between? What will you be learning in each subject? What skills will you be developing? What coursework will you have to do? How will you be tested in the examination?

About yourself
Which subjects are you good at? What are your particular strengths and skills? Which subjects are you interested in? Which subjects do you enjoy?

About careers
What types of jobs are available in the career areas that you are interested in? What qualifications do you need for those jobs?

STEP 2
– Consider the consequences

- of choosing a subject you do not particularly like because it is a subject that is needed for lots of careers. Would it be worth it, just to keep your options open?

- of cutting down the amount of science you do, to enable you to do another subject. Is it too risky, because you may change your mind and decide later that you want a scientific career?

- of starting a second modern language. Does it mean you would have a rather unbalanced course, because you would not be able to do a creative arts subject?

- of having to choose between two subjects you would really like to do because they clash on the timetable. What would be the consequences for your future choices, if you dropped either of them?

- of starting a vocational course. Would it provide you with extra skills? Would it offer you more of a choice at 16+?

STEP 3
– Ask about alternatives

- if you are stuck because your teachers are advising you not to drop a subject that you are good at. Is there a way of doing the subject you want as well as the one the teachers think you should do?

- if you are stuck because you cannot make the subjects you want to do fit into the option blocks. Is there an alternative way of making them fit?

- if you really are going to be forced to drop one of the subjects you would like to continue doing, ask if there would be an opportunity to take up the subject again at a later stage e.g. in the sixth form or at college.

STEP 4
– Double check

Show your options form to your parents or to your form teacher. Ask them to check that you have filled it in correctly and that you have really made the choices that you want.